WAITING ON WONDERS

40 DAYS OF WONDER DEVOTIONAL

TARA L. BANKS

Cover & interior design by Typewriter Creative Co.
Cover illustration by Carrie Davis @carriedavisart
Photo by Ellen Everson @ellencharisphoto

Scripture quotations marked NLV are taken from the New Life Version, Copyright © 1969 and 2003. Used by permission of Barbour Publishing, Inc., Uhrichsville, Ohio 44683. All rights reserved.

Scripture quotations marked (NIV) are taken from the Holy Bible, New International Version®, NIV®. Copyright © 1973, 1978, 1984, 2011 by Biblica, Inc.™ Used by permission of Zondervan. All rights reserved worldwide. www.zondervan.comThe "NIV" and "New International Version" are trademarks registered in the United States Patent and Trademark Office by Biblica, Inc.™

Scripture quotations marked (NIrV) are taken from the Holy Bible, New International Reader's Version®, NIrV® Copyright © 1995, 1996, 1998, 2014 by Biblica, Inc.™ Used by permission of Zondervan. All rights reserved worldwide. www.zondervan.comThe "NIrV" and "New International Reader's Version" are trademarks registered in the United States Patent and Trademark Office by Biblica, Inc.™

Scripture quotations marked (AMPC) are taken from the Amplified Bible, Classic Edition (AMPC) Copyright © 1954, 1958, 1962, 1964, 1965, 1987 by The Lockman Foundation.

Scripture quotations taken from the (NASB®) New American Standard Bible®, Copyright © 1960, 1971, 1977, 1995, 2020 by The Lockman Foundation. Used by permission. All rights reserved. www.lockman.org"

Scripture quotations marked (NLT) are taken from the Holy Bible, New Living Translation, copyright ©1996, 2004, 2015 by Tyndale House Foundation. Used by permission of Tyndale House Publishers, Carol Stream, Illinois 60188. All rights reserved.

Scripture quotations marked (TLB) are taken from The Living Bible copyright © 1971. Used by permission of Tyndale House Publishers, Carol Stream, Illinois 60188. All rights reserved.

Scripture quotations marked (MSG) are taken from THE MESSAGE, copyright © 1993, 2002, 2018 by Eugene H. Peterson. Used by permission of NavPress, represented by Tyndale House Publishers. All rights reserved.

Scripture quotations marked (ESV) are from The ESV® Bible (The Holy Bible, English Standard Version®), copyright © 2001 by Crossway, a publishing ministry of Good News Publishers. Used by permission. All rights reserved.

Scripture quotations marked (NKJV) are taken from the New King James Version®. Copyright © 1982 by Thomas Nelson. Used by permission. All rights reserved.

Scripture quotations marked (NCV) is taken from the New Century Version®. Copyright © 2005 by Thomas Nelson. Used by permission. All rights reserved.

Scripture quotations marked (VOICE) are taken from The Voice™ The Voice Bible Copyright © 2012 Thomas Nelson, Inc. The Voice™ translation © 2012 Ecclesia Bible Society. All rights reserved.

979-8-9874704-1-1 (Paperback)
979-8-9874704-3-5 (Hardcover)
979-8-9874704-0-4 (Jacketed Hardcover)
979-8-9874704-2-8 (eBook)

For Greg, who helps me keep the wonder alive.

The Lord is good to those who wait for him,
to the soul who seeks him.
—

LAMENTATIONS 3:25 (ESV)

CONTENTS

INTRODUCTION

T ucked inside the ordinary moments of life are wonders waiting to be discovered.

While often overlooked, the mundane holds miracles that can draw our attention to God—where we can hear Him speak and experience the wonder of His presence. This 40-day devotional is a collection of purposeful pauses to help us do just that. It's here in these "everyday Tuesday" kinds of moments where I've been waiting for you to join me, so we can walk together to find Him, hear His voice, and gain a greater awareness of His presence in our daily lives.

I'm so glad you're here.

For as long as I can remember, I've loved music. As a worship pastor for over 20 years, I've loved hearing the Lord speak through those thunderous worship moments with other believers, where it seemed heaven was so close you could walk right in. So, a few years ago, when the Lord asked me to purposefully turn down the volume of my life, give my soul space to breathe, and start getting really quiet to find Him, I wasn't sure I could hear the Lord clearly without all the noise. However...

I started finding the Lord in the tiny pauses of life, the normal, everyday quiet moments I was used to blowing right through in pursuit of the louder ones. I began to ask Him, "Right here, right now, what do you want to teach me?" And you know what? He started showing me precious little everyday things that have become the foundation of *Waiting on Wonders*.

I still love those thunderous worship moments, but now He is teaching me the sacredness of the silent pauses. I'm learning to embrace waiting on my faithful Father as He retunes my heart to sing His praise in the spaces in between. I'm seeking out those tiny pauses tucked within big *and* small moments. This is where the Lord's fingerprints can be found and what we'll find together as "fellow Wait-ers."

I remember becoming aware of one of those tiny pauses when I took my firstborn to kindergarten (UGH). I felt sure my heart would burst through my skin, even as I did my best to keep it together, take the obligatory pictures, and try not to think of his looming college application deadlines. Hand in hand, I led him to the door, gave him a big hug, held back all the tears, and watched him walk right on into a whole new world.

Did you see it? In that event that every parent experiences, there was a moment worth marking, a wonder worth waiting on.

It wasn't in the pictures I captured that day. The most important moment was the millisecond pause between holding his pudgy little hand tightly in mine and when my brain told me to stop squeezing and let his hand go, to let him walk through the door.

Right there. Pause.

If that event could have been played in slow motion, as distance was created between our outstretched hands, we would have seen the everyday moment where God was meeting me. He was with me, waiting for me, wanting to teach me more about Himself, and offering to hold *my* hand tight when it was time to let my son's go. He wanted me to be aware of His presence right then and there and hear His voice.

In that pause, He helped me understand that He loved me and that He had an entire lifetime of incredible plans for my son's future—and even though this was hard, it was right, and it was time to let go.

It was in that kindergarten hallway where I realized that in everyday moments, God was speaking. I just needed to wait long enough to recognize the wonder of His presence and hear what He wanted to say *to me*.

That's what *Waiting on Wonders* is all about.

HOW TO USE THIS BOOK

In the Bible, 40 is a significant number. Typically, it is representative of a time of trial or testing. It can also be a period of wandering or transformation. Regardless, it's a season of learning. You might be in the middle of a trial or shouting a testimony of what God has just brought you through. No matter your circumstance, He wants to meet with you in these next 40 days and create a season of wonder as you pause daily in His presence to listen for His still, small voice.

This devotional consists of simple reflections where I've stopped to notice God's presence in life's little pauses. Each devotion has a "How We Wait Today" prompt where we can open our hearts to how He might be speaking that day. The ✨ icon is a visual representation of a moment where you might want to wait, listen, and ask the Lord what He wants to say. It's my version of what the Bible calls "selah." Then, at the end of the week, there is journal space to make notes on what He said, how you saw Him move, and what He taught you. Simple.

Take it at your own pace. The goal is not to finish on time but to experience His presence in purposeful pauses along the way.

They all matter. Every strategic, epic, ordinary, long, microscopic, fabulous, normal moment. For these next 40 days, let's commit not to rush any of them. Instead, let's walk arm-in-arm and pause to hear God's voice as He leads us through.

There are wonders to be found as we wait on Him. "Be still before the Lord and wait patiently for Him..." Psalm 37:7 (NIV).

I'll be waiting with you,

Tara

WEEK 01

EVERYDAY WORSHIP

DAY 01 | YOUR WALKING-AROUND LIFE

So here's what I want you to do, God helping you:
Take your everyday, ordinary life—your sleeping, eating,
going to work, and walking-around life—and place it
before God as an offering.

—

ROMANS 12:1 (MSG)

God wants to meet with us in our everyday, ordinary, walking-around life. While folding laundry. While in the carpool line. While talking with a friend over coffee. And because He is a loving, relational, personal God, He longs for us to experience His presence and to meet us in our every day—the great, the messy, the terrific, and the terrible. And He can use those everyday moments to get our attention to remind us that He is real, He is speaking, and He loves us.

Our normal walking-around life can be worship if we recognize His presence and choose to be aware that He is with us as we go about our day.

Worship is what we were created to do, and in essence, it's like breathing back to God a life that honors the breath of life He breathed into us.

As with any skill, you must practice in order to feel comfortable doing it. You practice the piano to feel comfortable playing with ease. You practice driving to not have a wreck. (Pray for us. We have a new driver in our house again...yes, Lord). It is no different with God's presence. Getting comfortable in God's presence is not hard; it is just a discipline to be developed.

One of my favorite books about God's presence is *The Practice of the Presence of God*, written by Brother Lawrence, a lay Brother in a Carmelite monastery in Paris in the 1600s. It's a tiny book of letters about learning to experience God's presence in everything we do.

He beautifully says that practicing God's presence is simply the discipline of remembering that He is always with us and choosing to focus our soul's attention on Him.[1]

✦ It's a choice to engage His presence.

The more we are aware of His presence in our everyday, ordinary life and then practice recognizing it in those normal kinds of moments, the more we are comfortable being in it and experiencing all He has to offer there.

And best of all, He will begin to speak to you through those very normal things, and you will learn to recognize His voice more clearly.

We can choose to do whatever we are doing, as unto the Lord, in an effort to say, "In this moment, I want to be aware of your presence."

Every moment can be a holy one. Not just in church or on the weekend. But even a regular Tuesday.

Because He promises His presence is with us all the time, we can rest assured that we don't have to beg Him to come. However, it is a decision we consciously make to engage our hearts with His and to be aware He is there and how He is working and moving.

Whether at the grocery store as you speak to the cashier, when you see that sunset over the mountain or the marsh, or when everything seems to be falling apart, it's the discipline of recognizing His presence in those moments that changes everything.

✦ HOW WE WAIT TODAY

Practice His presence by recognizing Him in your everyday moments. Allow the normal things to become a path to His presence by choosing to acknowledge that He wants to speak to you in it all. It's not a matter of "Is he speaking?" It's a matter of "Are we listening?" Let's be found listening today.

---

(1) Lawrence, Brother, *The Practice of the Presence of God* (New Kensington, PA: Whitaker House, 1982), 66.

The Lord replied, "My Presence will go
with you, and I will give you rest."

—

EXODUS 33:14 (NIV)

When needing to recall something, typically, we have to stop and think for a moment. In the same way, when we need to remind ourselves of something God has said or done in the past, it's a great practice to stop and reflect. And often, we have to get quiet to focus. When we get quiet, it gives us the needed soul-space to be grateful for what He has done and recognize how His presence has been with us.

The world assaults us with noise and hustle, and I believe we need to turn our lives down—our phone, our social media, our calendars, our extra. If we want to get serious about hearing the Lord and to be reminded of all He's done, we've got to embrace quiet and a bit of SLOW.

If we want to go deeper in our relationship with the Lord and experience His presence more deeply, that does not come in microwaveable pouches. That is done slowly, over time, and with intention. The only way to live with intention, and on purpose, and to experience God's presence purposefully is to do it slowly.

Fast is the enemy of deep. You cannot run fast in deep water. In the same way, you cannot know the Lord deeply in two minutes. Deep takes time.

Throughout this book, you will find stories and examples of waiting to hear God's voice in tiny moments. Before we get there, let's talk about how to find them.

For the remainder of this week, we are going to pause and practice His presence by going slow. There are many ways to experience God's presence, but we'll use the acronym **SLOW** to give us an easy way to remember the moment-by-moment process:

STOP **L**ISTEN **O**BSERVE **W**AIT

Today, let's focus on STOP.

Stop. In the Greek, that means "stop." Seriously though, it's very self-explanatory. The likelihood of you having a deep encounter with Jesus when your life is at 100 mph is pretty unlikely. The life of Jesus was characterized by a slow, purposeful, interruptible, "unforced rhythms of grace"[1] kind of life.

To enjoy His presence, we must keep pace with the Lord, not outrun Him. You are going to need to physically stop. Stop scrolling. Sit down, breathe in and out, and let God speak to you. In the moments we purposefully stop and choose to focus our soul's attention on Him, we are reminding ourselves that He is with us. This, too, can be a holy moment.

Mamas, I get it. I'm a mama, too. I think my babies were 16 and 10 before I ever sat down. But, stop. Your family, your babies, your job, your heart, and your soul are crying out for you to get still. It's in that still place where the Lord is patiently waiting. Don't get me wrong, stillness doesn't mean doing nothing for a long time; it means doing things with a still spirit. It's letting His presence give you rest.

In Exodus 33, Moses is given the enormous task of leading the people out of Egypt—over one million of them. You can imagine that he was probably *just* a little busy with all those people and all their issues and all their complaining, while trying to get them to the promised land. And right in the middle of that chaos, God promised Moses that His presence would give him actual rest. So, nobody can tell me you're too busy to let God's presence give you *rest*. More than likely, none of you are in charge of one million people—even though it might feel like that on a Monday morning.

To fully experience God's presence, we must stop what we're doing and allow His presence to revive our souls with rest. When we do, and the sediment in our soul has time to settle out[2], we can see and hear the Lord more clearly. When our souls are quiet, His voice will become very loud, very quickly. This is where He longs to meet us today.

✦ HOW WE WAIT TODAY

Simply make a purposeful stop. Allow God's presence to give you the rest you need. When you feel your day spinning, or you are lost in some endless scroll on social media, stop. Take a deep breath and ask the Lord to speak to you in that very moment. Pause and let Him assure you with His presence.

---

(1) Matthew 11:28–30 (MSG).
(2) Barton, Ruth H., *Invitation to Solitude and Silence: Experiencing God's Transforming Presence* (Downers Grove, IL: InterVarsity Press, 2004), 29-30.

DAY 03 | LEARNING TO LISTEN

Today, if He speaks, hear His voice.

—

PSALM 95:7B (VOICE)

When we finally stop and get to a place where the sloshing of our souls subsides and our souls get still, this is where we can step into the next practice of choosing to daily slow ourselves down, to pause and experience His presence and LISTEN.

While we can experience His presence at any point in our day, one way we can be sure to hear His voice is to spend focused time reading the Bible. He speaks like He reads. Engaging the Scriptures daily is the primary path to His presence and to hear His voice. Choose one verse and ask God what He wants to say to *you* about it. Don't read what other people think about that verse or what social media says. Ask God to speak to *you*. In time, choosing one verse will turn into a greater hunger for His Word, and you will naturally want to read your Bible more. That's just how it works. You can be sure He will speak to you there.

If you are new to the Bible and you don't know where to start, that's totally fine. You are absolutely welcome here. Start in the book of John. It's the story of our friend, Jesus, and His life, and it will change yours as you get to know Him. The more we engage the Scriptures, slow down and listen, the more we will learn His voice.

The volume of His voice is directly proportional to the stillness of the soul.

And yes, you've been given everything you need to hear His voice. If you have ears and a brain between them, you can hear God speak!

I encourage you to find a translation of the Bible that you really connect with. There are over 400 English translations of the Bible. I'm old school and love a real-live paper Bible that I can mark up and track the hand of God in my life over time, through joy and sorrow. I enjoy translations ranging from word-to-word all the way to a paraphrase and will often cross-reference verses and translations to help me learn. Every 8–10 years, I feel a tug to buy a new Bible in a new version. It's hard to give up my "old faithful," but it comes with an excitement that I will learn and hear from the Lord in the familiar passages, in a new way, with fresh eyes. If you prefer digital, you can read the Bible online or in an app with dozens of translations available. No matter the medium, find a solid translation that you love and devour it. Don't be afraid to write in it or digitally highlight it. All of that is part of the listening.

When I slow down and prepare to listen to the Lord speak, sometimes I like to say aloud in a prayerful way, "I'm listening." This is not only accountability for my mind to key into what I think God might want to say, but to tell God that I'm choosing to be available in that moment. I'm choosing to let that everyday moment become a holy one as I choose to acknowledge His presence in it. Then, I open the Bible and see what He wants to say.

Remember, being in His presence, practicing hearing from Him, and experiencing Him every day is a choice. Choosing to take time to read His Word is always time well-spent.

✦ HOW WE WAIT TODAY

As we pause to listen for His voice, engage the Scriptures in your waiting. Better yet, begin to memorize verses so you can recall them when you need them. Getting God's Word deep in your heart is one of the best things you can do to learn to recognize His voice. Allow time in God's Word to help you slow down to retune your heart to the melody of His presence.

DAY 04 | LEARNING TO OBSERVE

Come close to God, and God will come close to you.

—

JAMES 4:8 (NLT)

W e can experience God's presence in our everyday moments as we stop, listen—and today, OBSERVE. This practice involves looking around your daily life and seeing where God might speak to you.

Are you sitting alone at a coffee shop listening to a podcast? Maybe God wants to teach you about silence and solitude and how Jesus regularly pulled Himself away to quiet places to pray.

Are you outside watching the kids play in the driveway? What in their playtime could be used to teach you? What does He want to say about you watching them like your loving Heavenly Father watches over you?

To "observe" is to simply be wide awake to God's presence.

Have you ever gotten a different car and suddenly you were more aware that other people had it too? You never noticed it before, but now that car is *ev-er-y-where.*

It's like that with practicing God's presence. Once you choose to focus your attention on Him, you start seeing Him everywhere and in everything.

Let's refocus our eyes. Open our hearts. Lift our heads.

In his beautiful book, Brother Lawrence insisted that to be constantly aware of God's presence, it was necessary to form the habit of continually talking with Him throughout each day.[1]

This is what "observe" is all about. Look at your everyday Tuesday life and talk to God about it. It's that simple.

"Hey God, I really love this mug that Jan gave me. Thank you for her. Will you bless her right now?"

"Ah. I see that little butterfly that just came by the window. Thank you for your creation and for bringing it my way, so I could see it. It's beautiful, and you're an incredible artist."

"This small human who lives in my house and keeps calling me, "Mom," is really testing me today. Help me to be grateful for him right now and remember these days will be gone too quickly, because I feel frustrated and don't want to waste this moment feeling that way."

It's an ongoing conversation about everything—and choosing to sense God's presence in it all.

Simply talk to God. Maybe it's in your mind. Maybe it's out loud. (But you might want to let people know you're not talking to them.) Regardless, open your eyes to His presence and then open your mouth to share it with Him.

Allow God to be a part of your every day. He is not surprised by all the beauty *and* all the broken things. On the contrary, He loves it all and wants you to share it with Him.

✦ HOW WE WAIT TODAY

As you lift your eyes in your everyday Tuesday kinds of moments, raise your awareness of His presence in the extraordinary and the uneventful. He is in it all. He wants to intersect our lives throughout our days to help us experience His great love for us. Let's not miss it.

---

(1) Lawrence, *The Practice of the Presence of God*, 11.

DAY 05 | LEARNING TO WAIT

Rest in the Lord and be willing to wait for Him.

—

PSALM 37:7A (NLV)

I don't know anyone who likes to wait. And when you read the title of this book, *Waiting On Wonders*, did you respond the same way? I don't want to wait, and if I did, why would I want to do it for 40 days?

This week, we've been practicing going SLOW as we've learned to: Stop, Listen, Observe, and today, WAIT. For those who have made it to Day Five, thank you. This journey will change how you experience the Lord. He loves you so much and wants you to enjoy waiting on Him. Learning to wait on the Lord is how we keep our expectations high, a 10 out of 10, for Him to speak to us in our everyday lives.

I get it. In a microwave world, we want it all right now. But to wait on the Lord is not the same as waiting on your seven-year-old to find their shoe. Lord, help the child.

We usually wait on the Lord in two ways. The first is with joyful expectation. An "edge of your seat" kind of waiting. Like, you can't wait to see what He's up to.

The second kind is another kind of "edge of your seat" waiting, but this time it's because you can't figure out why God is not on the edge of His. He doesn't seem to have the same urgency you do, and His timeline seems off to you.

Both can be good. Both can lead us to a deeper place in our relationship with Him.

Waiting on the Lord looks like trusting Him with all the outcomes: the exciting ones and the unsure ones. Trusting Jesus is not about having all the answers and skipping along in life with Him unaffected. Instead, waiting on Him is a reminder to trust Him—not because I know the plan and the path ahead—but because I don't.

In His great love, He will gently carry my tender heart. He will welcome all of my questions and be present in all of my seeking.

I don't have to have everything figured out and know the answers to all the problems. All I have to do is keep my eyes focused on Him, and He will make my path straight as we navigate through anything unknown together. His presence is with me. I can be assured.

Trusting Jesus is walking—*not running*—hand in hand with Him.

It's keeping our eyes locked on *Him*,

not the dips in the road,

not the tigers that lie in wait to devour us just off the path,

not the torrents of rain that soak our souls to the bone,

but keeping our eyes locked on *Him*.

Before we know it, if we're waiting and walking with Him, we'll realize He walked every bit of the journey with us, His presence never left us. Then, we'll be able to look back and see all the wonders that we uncovered together along the way.

✦ HOW WE WAIT TODAY

As you pause to wait on the Lord in your ordinary moments, ask Him, "What do you want to teach me, right here, right now?" Then, keep your expectation on "10" that He will speak to you personally right in the middle of your circumstances.

Next week, and the weeks that follow, we'll be pausing in His presence in ordinary moments and applying all that we've learned about going SLOW as we do.

Fellow Wait-er, He is crazy about you. Don't ever forget it. He'll do anything to get your attention, to let you know He is real, and to show you that He loves you. So, keep your eyes open, your heart ready, and be willing to wait on the everyday wonders He can't wait for you to discover.

END OF THE WEEK PAUSE

*Where did you sense God's presence this week as you paused to go
SLOW (Stop / Listen / Observe / Wait)?*

_____

_____

_____

_____

_____

_____

_____

_____

_____

_____

_____

_____

_____

_____

_____

What did He teach you as you paused and waited to hear His voice?

What verse made you pause and think this week?

WEEK 02

WAITING
IN CREATION

DAY 01 | PRUNING AND PLUMERIAS

Then He who sat on the throne said,
"Behold, I make all things new." And He said to me,
"Write, for these words are true and faithful."

—

REVELATION 21:5 (NKJV)

The first time I remember the Lord speaking to me clearly in nature was all because of a plumeria tree.

Anyone that is around me long knows of my deep connection and love for the Hawaiian islands. My extended family has had the unique opportunity to live on the islands on and off for a number of years. On one of those visits, I decided to try to bring Aloha home with me, and I bought plumeria trees to grow in my yard. (Plumerias are as Hawaiian as Magnolias are to the South). With great hope, I brought home two very small thick green plumeria sticks and plunked them into two huge pots to watch them grow. For several years they did absolutely nothing. Just two thick green sticks in the dirt. I was faithful to water, bring the pots inside when it got cold, make sure they had sun...basically, baby them. About four years later (no, I'm not joking), they finally started to look like plants, and these sticks began shooting out leaves and, ultimately, plumeria flowers.

My precious plumerias have become part of the Banks family. For many years we (read: my amazingly patient husband) even went so far as to sink those pots in the ground during the spring right by the front door, pull them out, and put them into the garage when the weather became 'un-Hawaiian.' They are so large now it's not possible to move them, but I still protect them fiercely when the temperatures drop. They love the sun, and I love when they are in bloom and enjoy the fragrance when I pass by.

One spring a few years ago, I noticed there were fewer and fewer leaves as they all began to fall off. I searched the internet for information about what was happening to my trees. Then, my heart broke as I read it: "black tip fungus." The death of plumerias! I frantically began to spray them with everything prescribed and did all I could to save these precious plants. As a last resort, and on the advice of a plumeria specialist (yes, there are such people), I took a very sharp knife to my precious trees and did what was necessary. I cut off each limb systematically. I cut off all the remaining brown leaves. I cut off the ends of every stem.

I cut each branch until white sap ran from the deep scars. The black tip fungus was, in essence, gone, but so were my beautiful plumerias.

I looked at my stubby, leafless trees and said, possibly dramatically, "You've been wonderful. Thank you for the joy you've brought to my life...goodbye." I thought, for sure, there was no hope. Nothing beautiful could ever come from them again. So, I left them in the ground, with little hope, in their pots to die.

Fast forward two weeks...I stared in amazement as fresh, green life bumps began to appear where the deep black scars ended on each stem. Forward two more weeks...amazed again. Tiny, tiny leaves began to form, and in two more weeks...lots of leaves, and as if by sheer "you aren't going to take me" kind of iron will, *branches* started forming from each cut to enable more leaves, more branches. Against all odds - spectacular growth! The plumerias not only were back but were fuller, more vibrant, stronger even...despite the terrible wounds. They were better than they ever were. Miraculously, life had returned to these plants.

What's the point of this horticultural tale? As I was walking by the plants soon after, the Lord, in a tough-love kind of way, spoke to me and said, "In the same way you essentially wrote off these trees in their most vulnerable state, aren't you glad I loved you too much to write you off when you looked the same?"

(- Ouch -)

And so, the pauses began.

The Lord used something very normal in my life to speak to me very clearly.

This was the first "wonder" in a list of many down through the years that He would use to help me hear His voice. This is where the book first got started in my heart all those years ago.

That pause was very convicting for me that day and awakened me to the reality that He was always speaking. He can use anything to get our attention if we are willing to slow down long enough to listen.

As I recovered from the painful yet true word He gave me, all the parallels started flooding my mind:

The deep wounds that had to be inflicted on the trees to make them bloom again—and—the deep purposeful wounds of Christ's pruning tool of discipline or trial needed to make all things new in my own life.

Me, leaving the plants to die and losing all hope—and—being guilty of leaving friends in their struggles rather than getting in there and helping them sort through them on their way back to the cross.

In this pause, He also reminded me of times I'd been deeply wounded for "pruning" sake, when areas of my life weren't growing the way He wanted, and He had to systematically take them out. Or times when I resisted in obedience and had to learn the hard way. He reminded me that even though those situations, seasons, or years were incredibly difficult, they brought me to a place that was so much more beautiful than the previous place I had been. And during those times when I felt lost, without hope, ugly, broken, and like I would never bloom again—I did.

Can you relate?

✦ *Sometimes, the terrible, hope-threatening, severe wounds in our lives can produce the kind of stunning growth He's after.*

Does He enjoy the pruning process? I don't think so, no more than I enjoyed taking that knife to my beloved trees. But I do believe He knows its necessity and looks on that process with love.

He has a love that sees the growth of our lives in a way that only He can. He sees what needs to be pruned for our good and His glory. A love that looks down from the cross and says, "I'm willing to take these wounds, die, and be "written off" by the world so that you might bloom in my abundance."

His love looks at who we truly are and who we can be, not who we've settled for and allowed ourselves to become.

✦ HOW WE WAIT TODAY

If you're in a season of pruning, just coming through one, feeling written off, or your life doesn't feel like it's in bloom, just know I've been there too, and we will all be there again. You are welcome here, pruning scars and all. Patiently wait for your cuts to heal. It's incredible what happens when He shows up and turns "nothing beautiful will ever come from this" into "something beautiful is coming, indeed."

DAY 02 | NATURE GETS IT RIGHT

*The heavens declare the glory of God, and the sky
above proclaims his handiwork. Day to day pours out
speech, and night to night reveals knowledge. There
is no speech, nor are there words, whose voice is not
heard. Their voice goes out through all the earth, and
their words to the end of the world.*

—

PSALM 19:1-4 (ESV)

Creation has this beautiful way of showing us how to worship and obey. It's simple. Creation's purpose is to give glory to God. It can't not. (It's worth the double negative.)

If you go to the most desolate and remote places on earth, there will be seeds waiting in the dust, ready to sprout with the first promise of rain. If you scale a mountain, there will be a flower blooming its heart out behind a boulder. Likewise, if you were deserted alone on an island (I certainly hope never!), you would find flora and fauna flourishing.

Just because. Just because that's what creation does. It glorifies God simply by fulfilling its purpose, no matter how basic.

Seeds in the dust will sprout.

Flowers will bloom behind the boulder.

Flora and fauna will reach toward the sky.

All in worship. All in an attempt to obey their Creator as He breathes on them, sets them into motion, and says *GROW.*

And they do. It's simple. They have one job...and they obey. In doing so, they are fulfilling their purpose and giving glory to God.

I'm constantly amazed at these small, uninstagrammed moments of obedience:

> The weed that pushes through the sidewalk again and again with an iron will. Ready to obey.

> The clouds that float by carrying their moisture cargo, ready to release when the Creator summons their surrender. Ready to obey.

> The moon that brings the tide and the waves that continuously crash through the dark of night. Ready to obey.

All of creation tuning their focus on their singular purpose: worship through obedience.

And the best part? None of it is done to be acknowledged. Weeds don't care about getting glory. Clouds don't care. Moon and waves don't care. They have one audience—one reason to do what they do. It's not for you and me to capture with filters. It's for their Creator alone. They are doing their version of "worship and obey." With all that they are, they are working to honor Him with what He's created them to do. Nature gets it right.

If they had eyes, they'd be glued to Him. If they had arms, they'd be outstretched. If they had voices, they'd be shouting at the top of their lungs.

They don't.

But we do.

In the same way that creation responds to its primary purpose, we are called to respond to our Creator in the way only we can as humans:

With our eyes fully focused on Him.

With our arms reaching for more in worship.

With our voices speaking and singing our declaration of love out loud.

Only we can worship Him in that way. The seeds and the clouds don't get that kind of honor. Only we get the privilege of using our bodies, voices, actions, and lives to worship Him.

Nature leads the way. We have much to learn from it about how our lives can point back to Him. Everything else in creation is already mid-song, so let's join the anthem and follow the example it gives to worship and obey with all we've got.

HOW WE WAIT TODAY

While it might be tempting to draw attention to ourselves, we are called to point every bit of focus to God as we do what we're created to do. God wants to use all of creation, us included, to show others how much He loves the world. Don't ever forget you are a part of what He created and has intended to use to point people directly to Him. Use your life today to point Him out well.

DAY 03 | WHEN IT STARTS TO RAIN

*For land that has drunk the rain that often falls on it,
and produces a crop useful to those for whose sake it is
cultivated, receives a blessing from God.*

—

HEBREWS 6:7 (ESV)

Have you ever had one of those days, one of those seasons, where it feels like, at every turn, it's raining? Things just don't seem like they are working out in your favor. Life seems extra. The car breaks just after the refrigerator goes out. Your phone took a nosedive on the sidewalk and now looks like a decoupage art project. It feels like life is brewing a giant storm just for you, and you are in the wrong clothes and without an umbrella. I've been there.

The reality is that we can't function without rain. If we don't experience a season of hard rain every now and then, things wither and dry up. If there aren't deep puddles, there is no deep soaking. Without rain, there isn't growth, and there isn't change. And while we wouldn't choose it, we actually need seasons of rain in our own lives where it seems like everything is getting soaked to do the necessary deep work in us.

Here's what I know about those soaky-seasons. It doesn't rain forever. Seasons of soaking are usually short-lived. And if there is indeed a flood of sorts, yes, it's devastating, but there is always a strengthening that comes after. There is always glory to give God when we recover and grow in a greater capacity—when we bloom into something more beautiful than we imagined we could.

Creation continues to be the best teacher. Recently, I was in a place where it rains Every. Single. Day. Sometimes it's just a mist, sometimes a deluge, but it's what makes that place so stunning. It's so green. Green doesn't happen without significant water. A significant soaking. Green in our lives, that kind of fresh-new-budding, containing-all-the-hope-of-spring type of green, usually comes after a really hard season of rain.

Are you in a season of deep soaking? Hang in there. You're just around the corner from the promise of green.

Rainy seasons of the soul are hard, but the seasons that cause the most significant growth are the ones that challenge us the most.

When you experience those times when it just rains and rains and rains.

When you're standing out in it, and the water runs down hard, and hair sticks to your face.

Those are the times.

If you're willing to surrender and let Him work in you, that's when it happens: growth.

In the same way that plants grow better when they recieve a long, hard rain instead of a light mist, a deep work in your spiritual life only comes from a long, deep soaking in the things of God. That journey to green takes time. If it feels like the bottom is dropping out and you're getting soaked to the skin, be reminded that what God is forming in you is for your good and your flourishing.

✦ HOW WE WAIT TODAY

If you are caught in a rainstorm, you have two choices. Either run for cover or embrace the deluge and make the best of it. It is going to rain. Life is going to soak us to the bone. How we allow the rain to help us grow is entirely up to us. So, if it's going to rain, you might as well have fun while getting wet. Run headlong into the soaking and watch the Lord bloom in you something truly beautiful. Here's to all of us on the journey to green.

DAY 04 | POTENTIAL

Now all glory to God, who is able, through his mighty power at work within us, to accomplish infinitely more than we might ask or think.

—

EPHESIANS 3:20 (NLT)

There was not much to it. It was a one-gallon, plain, black, contractor-grade plastic pot sitting on a clearance shelf at the back of the garden center. The tag said it was a giant hibiscus, but there was nothing evident that would make me believe it. I was taking the tag at its word.

At the end of the summer season, one of my favorite things to do is to go to the garden center and see what I can rescue and bring back to life. There have been more times than I can count that God has done the same for my broken heart or situation, so I like to return the favor.

The plant was on the clearance rack for a reason. It was barely alive; the roots were bound so tightly in the pot that it would hardly release. The dirt was dried out and falling out of its container. I put the plant in the ground beside the driveway at the corner of the house, hoping it would miraculously sprout into a beloved hibiscus bush. Fast forward a few weeks. Nothing was happening. It honestly still looked as dead as the day I brought it home. I resigned myself to the inevitable. It had only been a tiny investment, so I left it, and the seasons rolled on and winter set in. That would be that. Hibiscus plants don't do winter.

March appeared like a lion, and as the weather warmed, weeds began to sprout first in the yard. As I was pulling them out beside the driveway, I grabbed a small leaf that seemed different from the others.

Hold up. I know that leaf. That's a hibiscus leaf. Are you SERIOUS?!

One month later, that easily discarded, that barely recognizable iron-will plant was shoulder high on me, blooming and showing off the most giant 10" pink hibiscus blooms I'd ever seen. The same plant that had been left for the trash. The same plant that wasn't supposed to survive the winter. The same plant I completely neglected and left to the elements. The same plant I barely invested in.

It just needed someone to believe it had something left to give.

How shamefully true is it with us that we discard pieces of our own lives or the lives of others when we stop resembling what we were created to be? When we're left at the mercy of someone's selection or reduced to a label, that's when potential has the opportunity to come alive.

These days, this sweet plant, currently in its eighth season, incomprehensibly and entirely outside of its nature, blooms, dies, and returns each year just to remind me: He's in it all, and He alone is the authority on potential.

Sometimes, we just need to believe in the power of potential and what God can do through us. We need to look at ourselves and those we come into contact with, square in the eyeballs, and say, "Hey, you've got this. I know it doesn't look great now, but no winter of your soul will take you out. No back corner is too far for the reach and gaze of the Lord. He sees you and sees all you are capable of."

✦ HOW WE WAIT TODAY

Let's be that for one another, Kingdom people. Let's see those tiny blooms of purpose packed with the power to become. Call them out and cheer them on. Let's also be kind to ourselves. Instead of calling ourselves done before it's time, let's be willing to go to the forgotten places—find those unidentifiable characteristics and call them back to life. Even if we're stuck in our circumstances. Even if the potential you see still needs to be realized. Becoming is a process, not a one-time event. Let's be willing to give it time and watch it bloom, even in ourselves.

DAY 05 | WINTER'S WAIT

He has made everything beautiful in its time.

—

ECCLESIASTES 3:11 (NIV)

I'm a summer girl. I live in the deep southern part of the US for a reason—and somewhere around the beginning of March, I come alive. I come out from under the darkness of winter and step fully into the joy that, in Charleston, SC, it will be warm for the next eight or (if we're lucky) nine months.

Yes, I completely understand that a few below-40-frigid days in mid-January hardly constitute "winter" for most of the world, but when you grow up a summer girl, that is enough. To each his own.

There is much to be learned in the changing of seasons. As one shifts to the next, without permission or effort as it's done for centuries, creation submits to its Creator and accepts the process. Flowers begin to fade. Grass begins to go dormant. Leaves that started as tiny buds, months before, now begin their transition from green to yellow to red and every variation between. All growing things know it's their time to move on to the next season. As if an unheard heavenly declaration has gone out to proclaim, "Change is coming," it simply begins.

When winter has finally set in, the last leaves have fallen, the grass has died back, and, in some places, snow has started to fall, this is when creation has its most challenging work. It has to rest.

This doesn't mean that things aren't happening; it just means that much of creation is in a period of suspended animation, pressing pause on the growth that has been and will come. It's here in the cold earth where the seeds wait. It's here in the ground where the potential of spring is realized. It's here in the resting that creation stores the strength it will need for the next season.

In that resting, there is preparation. In that resting, every bit of what will be, lies in wait, ready to burst forth. And in that same way that it heard the call to rest, all of creation waits and listens for the call to go out again to come forth.

Somewhere deep in the earth, seeds stir. Roots shake off the chill of winter and stretch to strengthen the growth above ground. Spring is on the way, the silent signal has been given, and the earth comes back alive. Rested. Vibrant. Ready for another season of growth.

✣ *The winter season of our souls shouldn't be seen as a stopping place or where growth can't happen. Instead, these are the sacred places where the deep work is being done. In those waiting times, strength is stored up, and we're called to rest. It's not stopping the forward motion of what God wants to do in and through our lives; it's just a pause as we wait for all the potential.*

In the same way the seedlings are called to awaken from their slumber and burst forth into spring, so in our lives, we are called to rise from winter's wait into all God has for us. To become all we were created to be.

✣ HOW WE WAIT TODAY

What season is your soul in today? If you're in a season that's been challenging, and everything seems frozen-cold still, be reminded that all the beauty of the earth sits nestled beneath winter's quiet and is just waiting to show off in the spring. If it feels like the winter of your soul is still hanging on, be encouraged, growth will happen, seasons change, and so will this.

Are you in the middle of a time that feels like spring when you can sense God is doing something new? If so, soak up the growth to sustain you through the inevitable coming winter. Or are you nestled down in a season of rest, being strengthened as you wait in the protective covering of your loving Father who is preparing you for what's next? Winter is not death. It's just a time of waiting for the life that is to come. Fellow Wait-er, watch creation. Let it show us the way to respond.

END OF THE WEEK PAUSE

Where did you sense God's presence this week as you paused to go SLOW (Stop / Listen / Observe / Wait)?

What did He teach you as you paused and waited to hear His voice?

What verse made you pause and think this week?

PURPOSEFUL
PAUSES

DAY 01 | CHARACTER BUILDER

*Lord, teach me how you want me to live. Do this so that
I will depend on you, my faithful God. Give me a heart
that doesn't want anything more than to worship you.
Lord my God, I will praise you with all my heart.*

I will bring glory to you forever.

—

PSALM 86:11-12 (NIRV)

It's safe to say if you're reading this book, you want to be "good people." None of us aspire to be divisive or create purposeful chaos. But, we also don't accidentally do these things either. You don't wake up one day, stretch, pet the dog, and then find yourself robbing a bank at 9:15 a.m. on the way to the morning playdate. Those sorts of life outcomes stem from a series of decisions.

While that's a wild example, we don't accidentally develop godly character, either. There are intentional decisions that we make. Moment by moment. Day by day. Over time. Each one leads us either toward or away from a deeper relationship with the Lord. Developing a more Christ-like life does not happen "all of a sudden." It comes with intention and is meant to be a becoming, not an arriving.

He is more concerned with our hearts than with us making history. He is much more concerned with what happens IN us than through us—although He wants to use both.

✦ **Our character will be defined and refined as much as we allow it to be—but make no mistake, it's developed in the secret place—not out in the open with all eyes on you. The hours of the unseen develop the deep things in us.**

The daily habits of faithfulness are where our character is sealed.

It tends to come in seasons. If you are in a season of:

Learning to serve - that's where character is built.

Learning to wait - that's where character is refined.

Learning to understand your calling - that's where character is challenged.

Learning to embrace perspective - that's where character is changed.

Learning to refine parts of who you are - that's where character is solidified.

So, how do we develop the kind of character God wants us to have? Repeat this list. Again and again. Amen.

These seasons of learning are cyclical, and so is our character growth. In those cycles, we learn to obey, and that obedience becomes second nature as we become more like Jesus.

In the Garden of Gethsemane, the choice for Jesus was difficult, but not one he hadn't made before. He was accustomed to regularly bowing His agenda to His Father. When the moment came to either hightail it and run to the hills or step into alignment with sacrificial surrender, His track record of obedience was as unblemished as His heart. The choice He made for you and me was certainly not easy, but it was consistent with His nature. Jesus did the same thing that He had done every day of His life. He said, "yes." Yes, to the heart of His Father. Yes, to loving heart, soul, mind, and strength. A deliberate, willful, conscious Yes that started falling out of His mouth before the foundation of the world.

Patterns. Habits. One foot in front of the other. Diligence. Everyday compliance.

That's where obedience matures and turns into growth, and character development actually happens. It rarely is in the massive moments; typically, that's just courage dressed up. Instead, it's the daily routine of doing the hard thing.

The no quit.

The early-morning discipline.

The late-night fervor.

That's where obedience looks like submission to the Father. That's where faith is worked out, and the Lord crafts the heart. That is where the steel enters your spine, and calluses form on your knees. That's where deep-rooted decisions are made.

When we are accustomed to abandoning our lives to Jesus in the very small, over and over, we develop muscle memory to relinquish the most critical moments to Him. That's where character is formed.

Don't disregard the daily. Miracles are waiting for you in the mundane.

✦ HOW WE WAIT TODAY

Pause and consider, who are you becoming? Look out over the arc of your life, at all that's been said and lived and whatever will remain. What do you see? Are there patterns, daily habits, and intentions leading toward growth? Are the practices you have in place today leading in the direction you want your life to go? May we be found becoming more like Him every day.

DAY 02 | GREATER GROWTH

"I am the true vine, and my Father is the vinedresser.
Every branch in me that does not bear fruit he takes
away, and every branch that does bear fruit he prunes,
that it may bear more fruit."

—

JOHN 15:1-2 (ESV)

Recently, I was away from home for a few days, and when I returned, spring had happened in a major way in my yard. Flowers had bloomed. Trees had budded. Grass that had been brown, had reemerged after a winter of sleeping. It was all very green, and very pollen-y, and very lovely.

At a distance, everything looked as if it was flourishing, but the closer I got to the grass, I could tell it wasn't as much grass as it was weeds.

Counterfeit growth. It was green, but it was not the green I wanted.

I got down on my knees and scrutinized what stayed and what needed to go. When you pull weeds, there is going to be some collateral damage. You are going to pull up some grass with the weeds. The reason, how-ever, those weeds are growing in that spot is that the grass isn't healthy enough to choke it out. So, it will be a stronger lawn if the weaker grass goes as well to make room for healthier growth. It's a necessary sacri-fice. Out, it must come.

And so, it is with us. We must be willing to step back, gain perspective on what the Lord wants to grow in us, get on our knees and scrutinize what stays and goes, and then begin the dirt-under-the-nails work of pruning what has to go. Sometimes that means taking out even some of the good things in our lives. This process makes room for the best things God has for us and what He wants to see bloom, grow, and flourish in us.

When I looked at the lawn with a careful eye, I saw what was happening. It's funny how it sometimes takes stepping out of a situation or, alter-natively, getting really deep into the details to see what is happening right before you. It's often the blessing of distance, time, or a season, that allows our eyes to finally focus on it and see it for what it is. Have you ever been there? If we take the time to survey the landscape of our growth, often we will see things that are worth cultivating and things that need to be weeded out—all for our good, all for our growth, all to make us more like Him.

✦ *Indeed, just because it's growing doesn't mean it's good for us.*

Sometimes, things have been growing wild in us, and those very things have tried to take root, wreaking havoc in our lives. These can be the "good" choking out the "best." We've settled for a fast-growing green, but it's one of weeds and shallow roots that will wither in the sun. It looks good at a distance, but up close, won't survive when life turns up the heat.

Only green that has been properly assessed and tended will produce the growth we desire.

Yes, Lord, may it be spring season in my heart, regardless of the calendar. As you wake the world to the promise of what's new, may it remind me to tend to my heart. Help me not to be afraid to get down in the thick of what's really happening in my soul, to be ruthless with that cultivation, and to get about the business of really turning into the version of me you desire.

✦ **HOW WE WAIT TODAY**

Even if it's not the start of spring when you read this, it can be spring in your soul. Are there areas that need to be carefully evaluated? Perhaps it's time to let go of something "good" to experience the "best" He has for you. Step into the promise of this spring of your soul with intention. Lean into Jesus. Take a closer look at your heart today as you take one step closer to Him.

DAY 03 | CITIZEN OF HEAVEN

But we are citizens of heaven, where the Lord Jesus
Christ lives. And we are eagerly waiting
for him to return as our Savior.

—

PHILIPPIANS 3:20 (NLT)

What does it mean to be a citizen? I've looked up several definitions and basically, it's aligning yourself with a place, in return for its accompanying freedoms, responsibilities, and rights.

Citizenship is a belonging. Sometimes, you're born with it. Sometimes, you purposefully choose to become like or to reflect the people or community you are a part of by learning that place's language, culture, history, and customs. The belonging comes with duties that a person chooses to take on.

If I was a natural citizen of Zimbabwe, I would be fluent in the native language; my dress would reflect the culture; I would know the history of the area where I lived; and I would participate in the customs and traditions of that country. It would be clear that I was from Zimbabwe, not from Japan or the United States.

In Philippians, the Apostle Paul calls us "citizens of heaven." It's purposeful that he doesn't call us citizens of the earth, even though this is where we live and work and rest and play. As citizens of heaven, it implies that we should take on the language, culture, history, and customs of heaven. Even though we were born here and will die here, we are not "from" here.

If we take on the language of heaven, we should not sound like we're from earth. Our speech and thoughts, and how we communicate with those around us should sound different.

If we take on the culture of heaven, we should look and dress and act differently. Our choices regarding what we listen to, read, watch, and participate in should set us apart.

If we take on the history of heaven, we should know the timeline of key events. We should understand the key players in the stories and our ancestral heritage. There should be a deep understanding of how our lives fit into the bigger picture and how we impact the next generation.

If we take on the customs of heaven, we should participate in the traditions steeped in time, and do so in a community of others practicing those same traditions. There will be activities and events ingrained in who we are as citizens that should distinguish us from others.

✦ *Being a citizen of heaven should mean we don't fit into this world. We are here instead to show the world what the Kingdom of Heaven is like. We are not to be exclusionary, but we are to be different.*

We are only living here for a short time, and soon, very soon, we'll be heading back to where our hearts can finally settle in. Earth is our ministry. Heaven is Home.

✦ HOW WE WAIT TODAY

It's tempting to forget that we are not from here. It's tempting to blend into the culture and be "so well-adjusted to your culture that you fit into it without even thinking" (Romans 12:2 MSG). How can you be mindful today to ensure your life is different and be set apart for your true heavenly citizenship? In light of that, and where we truly belong, how can you reframe your thinking to align with your true citizenship today?

DAY 04 | FOR HIS PURPOSE

"Please, Lord, I am not a talented speaker. I have never been good with words. I wasn't when I was younger and I haven't gotten any better since You revealed Yourself to me. I stutter and stammer. My words get all twisted."

—

EXODUS 4:10 (VOICE)

There are plenty of days when I have felt unqualified for one reason or another. You know the days—when you just don't feel like you fit the mold of what is needed or required of you. There have been times when I've felt:

Too young and too old

Too stoic and too emotional

Too much and not enough

However, when it comes to God's purposes and how He wants to use us, He can use all of what we view as lack and turn it into abundance.

Several times, the book of Exodus notes that Moses had some sort of speech impediment or difficulty speaking. In Exodus 4:10, Moses pours his whole heart out to the Lord and shares how he feels unqualified to rescue the people of Egypt, as the Lord has called him to do. Ultimately, he asks his brother, Aaron, to be his spokesperson.

Moses is my people.

On Oct 1, 2016, in a singular moment that could only be described as a miracle, I was healed from Lyme Disease after an 18-month battle. While the debilitating symptoms are no more, and I give God all the honor for that healing, I've been left with some mild neurological issues and a version of expressive aphasia. I know what I want to say out loud but often have trouble getting it out. I have learned to cover it up well. I use humor, exaggerated hand motions, or divert attention while my brain frantically catches up. To most, it's hardly noticeable. To me, it's embarrassing and frustrating. I'm not great "on my feet" and makes me admire those who can speak eloquently and off-the-cuff. Some people I've known my whole life don't know. Those that do will help to finish my sentences or patiently wait for me to get my thoughts together. This is why I write. All the thoughts that run through my brain but struggle to come out of my mouth are more easily put on paper when I have the luxury of a bit more time and a delete key.

Every now and then, God allows me to string important words together out loud to encourage someone or deliver what's on His heart for a person or situation. That's when I know it's genuinely from Him. Outside of His work in my mouth at that moment, I know it to be impossible. However, I have seen the Lord turn this "I'm not enough" into "I'll be all you need."

And as if to put an exclamation mark on this idea for me, He now has me using my words to write a book—on waiting—for all the times I've waited on my words to show up and fall out of my mouth. He's now giving me a chance to say them all on my own terms. What a precious Savior.

✦ **When you feel unqualified, remember that the Lord is simply looking for a vessel.**

I often forget this. I often think that I have to be all of it or nothing. Instead, He can use whatever is available: my youth or age, my serious nature or tears, my knowledge or lack thereof, all my words or none at all, to be the very thing to catalyze His purpose.

> *"Go now, and I will be there to give you the words to speak; I will tell you what to say."*
>
> —
>
> EXODUS 4:12 (VOICE)

Let Him use you today for His purposes.

✦ **HOW WE WAIT TODAY**

For the days when you sense that you are unqualified in some way, remember that the Lord is the one who defines your success—not man, not even yourself. He is the one who determines your steps and how He will use them for His purposes. There are stories upon stories in the Bible of people used by God outside of what would be expected of their age, capabilities, or circumstances: Moses. Abraham and Sarah. Gideon. David. Esther. Paul. Mary. God can use us all, and none are disqualified in the Kingdom of God. So pause today, consider where you are counting yourself out. Ask the Lord to help you change your perspective. Ask Him to help you see your situation as an opportunity to be used by Him.

Then a cloud appeared and covered them.
A voice came from the cloud. It said,
"This is my Son, and I love him. Listen to him!"

—

MARK 9:7 (NIRV)

Who are you? We are often tempted to answer this question with our names and what we do.

I'm Tara. I'm a wife to Greg, mother to Ethan and Brody, worship pastor, hunger fighter and writer.

It's not a bad thing to respond in this way, but it's only a very small description of who we are. When our identity is instead perceived through the lens of how Jesus sees us, we can be assured that we are not what we do. However, whoever we believe we are will determine how we live.

We cannot begin to walk in the fullness of our identity if we don't have a firm grasp on what we believe about ourselves and the Lord. This stems from knowing God's Word, listening for His voice, and believing what He says about us. If we don't know His voice, we will believe things about ourselves that are simply not true.

The Israelites knew what God could *do*, but Moses knew who God *was* because he talked with Him and listened to His voice!

Whose voice do you value?

I value my husband's voice. He is my favorite hello, and my hardest goodbye, and his voice on the phone or coming through the back door is like an oasis to me.

I value my best friend's voice. She lives in Georgia, and when I hear her on the other end of the phone, I know it will be a good day. She prays for me, makes me laugh, encourages me, and speaks the truth where I need to hear it.

I value my kids' voices. Even in a room full of people saying, "MOM," I know when it's my flesh and blood calling my name.

Of course, more than all, I value the voice of my heavenly Father and how He speaks over me. I'm learning to pause and hear Him more and more. But sometimes, I forget to listen to all He says about me.

I'm much more apt to listen to the voice of the enemy and let him define me, let him shape my identity. You know why? It's LOUD and, honestly, sometimes easier to receive. That's why we have to purposefully pause to shut out the noise and listen carefully for the voice of the Father.

It's the same with what we say over ourselves. If you believe it, you will begin to value it, and then begin to live that thing out.

When I was younger, my mother always declared over me as I left the house, "Remember who you are and who you represent!"[1] That applies when you're a 17-year-old heading out into the world or a grown woman searching for her identity in Christ.

✦ Don't forget whose you are when searching for who you are.

Do not let your identity be wrapped up in position. Your primary identity is in Jesus. Your secondary identity is whatever is in your hand. Your position is just where you are, not WHO you are.

Whose voice am I valuing? Am I believing what God says about me and putting all my value into that? No one can label you or tell you what you are becoming. Only Jesus can do that as He lovingly declares, "You are mine. You belong to me. And only I get to say who you are."

✦ HOW WE WAIT TODAY

Self-affirmations can seem a bit crazy, but when it's steeped in Scripture, it's absolutely appropriate to declare those truths over ourselves. When we draw on the authority of Scripture and the identity it declares over us as believers in Jesus, that informs our actions and beliefs. Surround yourself with other believers who will encourage you and remind you of your real identity when you forget. Fellow Wait-er, that's why we need to do this life together with people who are also on the journey of becoming. So pause today, reflect on the following Scriptures, and walk confidently in your identity defined only by your loving Heavenly Father: Ephesians 1:4, Romans 1:6-7, Galatians 4:6-7.

---

(1) This is still the best advice that Ganelle Roberts has ever given me. I love you, Mama. This one is for you.

END OF THE WEEK PAUSE

Where did you sense God's presence this week as you paused to go SLOW (Stop / Listen / Observe / Wait)?

What did He teach you as you paused and waited to hear His voice?

What verse made you pause and think this week?

WEEK FOUR

MIRACLES IN
THE MUNDANE

DAY 01 | BALANCING ACT

Because of the Lord's great love we are not consumed,
for his compassions never fail. They are new every
morning; great is your faithfulness. I say to myself,
"The Lord is my portion; therefore I will wait for him."

—

LAMENTATIONS 3:22-24 (NIV)

In 2020, many of us were forced to become homeschooling parents. (Wild applause for all the parents goes right here.) When my sons were much younger, there was a season that I was homeschooling them and also working a full-time job that I loved. Those days were filled with trying to balance family, work, school, sports, friends, church, and relationships, plus anything else the day brought. Some days, keeping all the plates spinning was doable. Others, it wasn't.

Welcome to a peek behind the curtain of my life. Here's a page from my journal from a very normal homeschooling day a few years back and what I learned in the pause that day.

Today was algebra and arguments. Negative numbers and negative attitudes. Flipping fractions and flippant words. The careful and the careless. The methodical and the messy.

Before I could even open my eyes today, I could already hear the imaginary plates breaking. I knew I had a full day of work and felt the weight of the day's plates beginning to stack as my waking thoughts raced with the mounting to-dos. I had barely had coffee when the first plate stopped spinning with an unexpected email. Then school started. We were knee-deep in all. of. it. with emotions high by 10 a.m. By 2:00 p.m., we had settled in a bit, but only after raised voices, reminders, and reconciliation. By 5:00 p.m., our pace was perilous. Rushing from this to that...all good things...all things we enjoy. But the pace. The pace. UGH. By 9:00 p.m., we were home, but the weariness from the day had set in so hard, it was as if we were looking for ways to offend and to be offended.

Right in the middle of the 13th argument of the night, that's when I heard myself say, "I just can't do all of this!" and as those words came out of my mouth, I knew a pause was coming as I heard all the imaginary plates shatter on the floor. So, I took a deep breath right there in the kitchen, and the Lord began to speak to my heart and said, "Who said you had to?"

And so - the pause.

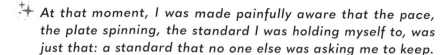 *At that moment, I was made painfully aware that the pace, the plate spinning, the standard I was holding myself to, was just that: a standard that no one else was asking me to keep.*

Sure, the world says, "Insta-compare myself to death with crafty excellence that my children will adore me for, serve the neighbor down the street a home-cooked meal after I have created a culinary wonder for my own adoring family, make my house look like I won every HGTV award, perfectly dress my kids, press my sheets, home school my children, be a full-time mom (read: don't you dare work outside of the house), and make sure I look like a supermodel while I am doing it, and...oh, and post it all on social media." (I smile sarcastically). Yes, this is what the world and all the outlets will tell me. *If I listen.*

Yes, those are all good, worthy, and honorable things; maybe one day I'll live up to them—or not. First, however, I have to make sure I'm asking myself, "Who in the world told me that?" Was that the voice of my loving Creator who sings His love and affection over me? The one who beckons me to come and sit at His feet? Certainly not. If it's not my Creator, then it's absolutely the voice of the world that wants me to compare and strive and hustle to some imaginary finish line that always is moving, while keeping all the plates intact.

Impossible.

So, I must learn to pause and regain His perspective over my life, not adopting one I've allowed others to dictate as the life I'm supposed to live.

I have to regularly pause to remember: the Lord is already pleased with me, whether I keep the plates spinning or not.

Fellow Wait-er, you are doing great—broken plates and all. You are not alone.

HOW WE WAIT TODAY

Today, if plates stop spinning, the world will not. And neither will the approval of the Lord. But, if the Lord allows, we will have tomorrow to try again and to purposefully pause, hear His voice, and give ourselves the grace He so freely offers, and we so desperately need. Let's focus on being grateful that His mercies are new every morning. Tomorrow, with renewed perspective, we can pick up fallen plates and give them to the Lord. Not only will He take those broken pieces and, no doubt, make them into something extraordinary, but He will also hold our faces in His hands and tell us, "I am Everything, so you don't have to be."

DAY 02 | THE END OF A SEASON

Whatever is good and perfect comes to us from God.
He is the One Who made all light. He does not change.
No shadow is made by His turning.

—

JAMES 1:17 (NLV)

Recently, my oldest son finished college. He did it super-speedy style in three years and in the middle of a pandemic. And while he wanted it to be over as quickly as possible, my husband and I were busy figuring out how to wreck the space-time continuum so that time would stand still. We were at the end of all the borrowed time we'd been given with our son. We knew the season would soon vaporize—and it did.

And just when I recovered from the emotional upheaval of college graduation, eighty-five short days later, that same young man held my hand, kissed my cheek, and sat me down on the front row of the best day of his life—as he promised his heart and vowed his life in marriage to his high school sweetheart. Once again, I felt as if I had been robbed by Father Time and was trying to grapple with the end of a season of our lives and how to "be" about it all.

We were thrilled! And stunned. And overjoyed! And our hearts were in 100 pieces and stuck in our throats. My husband and I stopped, shook our heads, stared at each other in amazement, and asked, "What just happened!?"

In wrapping up two monumental seasons, I have so many thoughts.

Should we be proud of what's been accomplished? You betcha. Should we feel shocked that the previous season is over and the next awaits? Totally. Should we feel sad and mourn the loss of what was? Indeed. Should we be grateful for all that was and what's to come? Completely. Should we be relieved that it's done? Yes. Concerned about the next season? Absolutely. And excited? Yes, so very excited.

Have you ever been at the end of a season or on the cusp of a new one and not known how to "be" about it? You are in great company.

I'm learning that our hearts can hold many complicated things at the same time. And I'm learning Jesus isn't afraid to walk right into all the raw and listen as we try to explain our tangled hearts to Him. He sits with us patiently as we choose His presence, and He gently pulls one thread at a time until the knots unravel.

✦ *Seasons. As they come and inevitably go, mark the tangled pieces with pauses. It's essential to unfold them with care, give them time, and let all the messy pieces have their moment.*

Will there be conflicting emotions? Yes. Is that part of it? Absolutely. But no matter if you're entering a new season, in the middle or at the end of one, be sure to stop and mark it. But mark every aspect with a spirit of gratitude—for what was, is, and will be. It will set your heart in the right place to enter the next season God has for you.

✦ **HOW WE WAIT TODAY**

Give your heart the freedom to wrestle down all the emotions and feelings of where you've been and where you're heading. No season of change is a surprise to the Lord, and as we pause and reflect in those moments, He will speak to us and guide us through. The Father waits patiently for us to be present in His presence and be reminded that though seasons change, He never does.

DAY 03 | YOUR LIFE IS A LIGHT

*The Lord gazes down upon mankind from heaven
where he lives. He has made their hearts
and closely watches everything they do.*

—

PSALM 33:13-15 (TLB)

On my most recent trip, I was flying on a particularly clear night, and I peered out the window and saw the lights of a city approaching. I could see the whole city, all the roads, communities, and buildings; it really was spectacular. I noticed how the streets connected, how the communities were laid out, and how the buildings were placed. Then, right there in seat 12A, I heard the Lord speak quietly to my heart as I watched the great big wide world go by.

"Every light is a story, and every story matters."

I looked closer and tried to focus on just one light...to find one light in a multiple of billions.

No matter how much that one light seemed to blend in with all the other lights at 10,000 feet, that light represented someone's story. That light represented someone's life.

That light was probably a streetlight in a neighborhood, which gave light to several houses. All with families in various forms. All with heartaches and joys, questions and trouble. Some with dinner on the table, some not. That light represented someone's dream of renting or owning a home. A place to come home after work and connect with those they love, or a place to go where there was no connection with anyone. It represented babies being born, people dying, and loved ones with great news to share or experiencing moments of absolute terror.

No doubt, all of those scenarios were happening in a city that size. All of it happening at the same time and creating a network of stories between strangers and families as it all came to pass. I was acutely aware that the triumph and tragedy of life was playing out right below me, yet I was busy at my cruising altitude, unaffected by any of it.

While I was passing by at top speed, not only was the Lord with me but simultaneously with each of those people as well. He was standing at their doorstep, sitting in their living room, kneeling at their hospital bedside, keenly aware of each and every situation and loving them as only He can.

Every life-light is a story. God knows every person their story reaches. Everything they feel. Every hair on their head. Everywhere in the world. All at the same time.

In that paused moment, the Lord encouraged me to shake off any tendency to cruise right on by people in my life. Too often, I've been guilty of being too busy with my own story instead of being mindful of what part He might want me to play in the story of others.

He reminded me through the visual of those lights that night how much people and their stories matter. He wanted me to slow down in that fly-by moment and remember that He loves them, too—more than I could ever imagine.

HOW WE WAIT TODAY

Throughout your day, remember those around you have a story, and their story matters, too. You might be just "flying by" their life, but don't be so involved in your own story that you're unaware of what He is doing in them. He just might want to use you to encourage them or point the way to Him. Or perhaps, you might feel like your life is only one tiny light on one tiny street in the middle of nowhere, and no one cares about or knows your light-story. Jesus does. He sees you and is with you and is writing a beautiful novel of your life. Your life is a story, and it matters.

DAY 04 | EVERYDAY PAUSES

This is the day that the Lord has made.
Let us rejoice and be glad today!

—

PSALM 118:24 (NCV)

There is a pause in the delivery room. It's in the seconds that elapse between the "It's a BOY!" and the first big cry. I'm pretty sure that's when it happens. That's when, as a mother, you hear the sound of your own heart learning to beat outside of your body.

Within those seconds, so many shifts occur. Your family grows. Your capacity increases. You become something you weren't before. What had been hidden and nestled deep for nine months becomes more real than ever. Those seconds change your life.

There's also a pause when you teach them to ride a bike. It's in the seconds after you take off the training wheels, give the back of the bike a little push, and they ride off down the sidewalk without you. I'm pretty sure that's when it happens. That's when, as a parent, you watch the little feet you made, carry them into a whole new world.

Within those seconds, there is more shifting. You are so proud. You are so sad. What had been a relationship between you and your little one is now going to be shared with new friends and people outside of your home. Those seconds form you.

There's a pause when you watch them struggle. It's in the seconds that elapse between the raised voices and pre-teenage sighs, and the "I'm sorrys" that are exchanged shortly after. I'm pretty sure that's when it happens. That's when you see the soul you desperately pray for wrestle with everything life is throwing at them.

Within those seconds, the shifts continue. You watch them become. They resent the becoming. You sense a natural and good, but hard and sad, beginning of the pull-away. Those seconds sting you and yet draw you to love them more deeply. Those seconds challenge you.

Then, there's a pause when they turn 18. It's in the seconds that elapse between "Good morning," and when you give a smiling, how-did-we-get-here, tear-streaked "Happy Birthday, Big Man," to your baby in a young man's body. I'm pretty sure that's when it happens. That's when you realize every awesome, awful, funny, painful, beautiful, broken, precious pause up to now has been leading to this one. Each has shaped him and has shaped you. And for a moment, in that pause, those same eyes that opened for the first time 18 years ago wake to the morning light, and in some sleepy, strange man-voice say, "Love you, Mama."

And that's when it hits you; all of life's best moments have happened in the pause.

Every pause is purposeful, and all the moments between them make a life. They are making up our "today." This is our real life, and we do not get another shot! Remember that while God is in life's big moments, He is just as active in the precious pauses creating miracles in the mundane.

HOW WE WAIT TODAY

No matter if it's a celebration day or simply a regular Tuesday, pause to find God and hear His voice. He will be in the seconds and moments between the big triumphs. He will be in the skimmed-over sections of your day. He will be in the hardly noticed parts of your afternoon. He will be in heartbeats and breaths in the blinks of an eye. So, take a mental step back and see where He might be speaking and how you can learn to find Him there. We can trust because He loves us; He is in them all.

DAY 05 | COMPARISON

This is where God comes in.
God has meticulously put this body together;
He placed each part in the exact place
to perform the exact function He wanted.

—

1 CORINTHIANS 12:18 (VOICE)

Today, I'm pausing in the produce aisle, and I'm thinking about comparison.

What if the strawberry says to the pepper, "I want to be you! You're so big and spicy and add so much life." Meanwhile, the pepper wishes it had seeds on the outside and juicy sweetness. Yet, if you replace a pepper in a recipe with a strawberry, it would be a disaster! And wouldn't it be awful if there were no strawberries? Or no peppers?

You know what? Not only do fruits and vegetables not talk, but this scene would never happen if they did. A strawberry plant grows strawberries to the best of its ability, no matter who is watching or what is growing around them, because that's what it was created to do. A pepper plant will grow peppers like crazy—not because it secretly wants to be a strawberry, but because it owns its Kingdom place. It's rocking the gift of being a pepper!

There are eight billion people on the planet. And right now, there is not another person on the planet with the same set of gifts, talents, and DNA as you. We can trust that God's gifts have been given to us specifically for such a time as this.[1] But, if we don't fully express them in only the way we can for this time in history, it is as if there is a gap in the Kingdom where those gifts should have been expressed.

In the language of 1 Corinthians, I can't be "the foot." You can't be "the arm." It's silly to compare ourselves to one another because we all serve different, yet specific, functions in the body.

Every gift given needs to be expressed to make the Kingdom whole. If we're busy comparing ourselves to others, or wanting someone else's gifts, or worse, trying to copy another person's gifts, that sadly leaves what God put in you, untapped.

So how do we combat comparison? We need relationships, a community to guard us against comparison. The enemy wants to isolate us so that his whispers alone become our companions. We need to link arms and be an encouragement for one another, cheering for—not comparing— the gifts and abilities that God has given us.

We need friendship and vulnerability. We need to be honest and say, "Hey, I've been through that minefield; let me help." Or, "Hey, I'm really having a hard time. Can you pray for me?" We need to help each other see ourselves the way the Lord does.

I can't be you...you can't be me. And that's fantastic.

I need you to be you. You need me to be me. I want the Kingdom to come and see Jesus completely glorified and receive everything He's due. For that to happen and for there to be no gaps, I need you to bring the full version of all you are to the table and express your gifts. I'll be over here doing the same. It's the ultimate "you be you" in the best way possible.

✦ HOW WE WAIT TODAY

It's easy to compare our life, home, children, marriage, or relationships to what we see on social media or with those around us. The next time you're tempted to lay down the beauty of who you are and what God has put in your life for such a time as this, be reminded that you are on this planet for a purpose. We need you. We need you to express all the beauty and specific nuances of your life to make the Kingdom all it can be. Fellow Wait-er, let's work today to be comfortable in our own skin with our specific gifts. Let's glorify the Lord with all we've got as we use every bit of it to seek Him.

---

(1) "And who knows but that you have come to your royal position for such a time as this?" Esther 4:14 (NIV).

END OF THE WEEK PAUSE

Where did you sense God's presence this week as you paused to go SLOW (Stop / Listen / Observe / Wait)?

What did He teach you as you paused and waited to hear His voice?

What verse made you pause and think this week?

PAUSES IN PERSPECTIVE

"I say this because I know what I am planning for you,"
says the Lord. "I have good plans for you, not plans to
hurt you. I will give you hope and a good future."

—

JEREMIAH 29:11 (NCV)

A few things make us distinctly Banks: the way we all cheer for different English Premier League soccer teams, the way we have a passion for all kinds of music, the way we love all things Aloha, and the way we consume zucchini bread. Yes, in our family, it's an art form.

One afternoon, many years ago, my youngest was helping me make that week's batch of zucchini bread. In the process of "assisting," he had spilled a bit of flour on the counter and was busy poking his chubby finger in his little mess, when he asked me if he could taste it. "Sure," I answered, pouring the last bit of batter into the loaf pans. "But it's not going to be as yummy as you think."

My little helper put his finger in the flour and straight into his mouth, thinking he'd surely be getting a treat. Instead, his little nose wrinkled up. He tried to muster an "mmm" sound, pretending he had made the right decision. I laughed because it was oh-so-precious, and then handed him a huge spoon. I'd already planned to let him lick the batter bowl—by far, the best part. With sparkling eyes, he grabbed the spoon, scraped the bowl clean in a matter of seconds, and said, "Thank you, Mommy!" Then, he climbed down from his kitchen-chair perch, with the remnants of the batter all over his face and hands.

And that's when it hit me. The pause. Isn't that like us with the Lord?

Our loving Father has amazing plans and dreams for us. But, instead of waiting on Him to receive them at the right time, we ask Him, as we poke our chubby little fingers in our own messes, "Can I have this?" All the while, He's got a yummy concoction of a plan just around the corner that would be so. much. better. than we could ever imagine if we would only be willing to wait on Him for the better thing.

✦ **Nonetheless, He says to us in love and with a heaping cup full of mercy, "Sure, beloved, you can have your little mess, but it's not going to be as yummy as you think…"**

Then, once we've tasted that experience and it has left us feeling less than satisfied, He often surprises us with something even more incredible. (And this is after we've pretended that we had the better idea!) Out of His great love for us, and without a drop of condemnation, He longs to offer us His best plan, His highest will for our lives. Unexpected blessings.

✦ HOW WE WAIT TODAY

Precious, gracious Father, how I long to be like my batter-covered boy having the remnants of your blessings all over my life. Help me learn to not settle for the mess I create, but to be willing to wait for the chance to lick the bowl of all you've got for me. Amen.

DAY 02 | KEEPING THE WAVES AT ARM'S LENGTH

The followers came to awake Jesus. They said, "Teacher! Teacher! We are going to die!" Then Jesus got up and spoke sharp words to the wind and the high waves. The wind stopped blowing and there were no more waves. He said to them, "Where is your faith?" The followers were surprised and afraid. They said to each other, "What kind of a man is He? He speaks to the wind and the waves and they obey Him."

—

LUKE 8:24-25 (NLV)

One of my favorite places to go is the beach. Like I mentioned, I'm a summer girl. It's unlikely you will ever see my favorite beach in any travel magazine or internet search. It is a private section of beach off the beaten path, where you only find footprints of birds and the scurry marks left by ghost crabs. There is a shallow reef, about ¼-mile offshore, where distant waves crash. On shore, the crystal blue water reflects the sky and laps quietly on the beach. As an introvert, it truly is my happy place. (And no, I'm not telling you where it is).

This is also where I have been fortunate enough to have heard the Lord speak to me very clearly. One afternoon, he began to speak to me about how those far-off violent, thundering waves contrasted with the quiet lapping of water right at my feet.

He said, "It's the same water; it's up to you how you experience it."

One was in tumultuous chaos. One in a peaceful release. Same water—only ¼-mile difference—but two distinct experiences. It was a tiny pause where I heard His voice, which significantly impacted my perspective.

Have you ever gone running on the beach? How about in waist-deep water? Same action, two totally different experiences. Similarly, there have been so many times when I've gone sprinting out into the ocean of my trouble to try to rush in and "fix something." I soon realize that running into the deep water of my panic and impulse is difficult and ineffective. The faster I try to run into the ever-deepening water of chaos, the harder it is. My feet lose the ground in confusion as I get in over my head, exhausted by my own doing. Time and time again, I wind up treading water in my circumstance, finding myself defeated and overwhelmed.

And yes, while the Lord certainly wants me to acknowledge the trouble or chaos and not deny it, He simply calls me to stand at a distance and name the moment for what it is, and then ask for His help rather than to dive in and try to command the ocean on my own. Instead, keep it at arm's length.

From the safety of the shore, He desires for me to watch from a protected distance as He handles the issue, the problem, the chaos...in love. He wants me to learn to trust Him.

I can still tell the waves of my trouble are big, but not NEARLY as big as they would be if I were at the foot of them, experiencing them crashing down on me.

Instead, I can experience those waves from arm's length. When the water of the trial reaches me, and it will, I know it has been filtered through His hand and protection. From that vantage point, I can respond more appropriately and learn to trust Him.

It still impacts me, but differently. Less panic. More peace.

Life is hard. Waves of trials surge without warning. But our perspective can change everything. The Lord wants to act as our buffer and place of safety. Either I can run straight to Him, or I can run straight for the chaos and make it worse. No matter what tsunami comes, my God is still bigger and loves to speak to the waves of my situation and tell them to chill out. So, when faced with a problem, I now ask: Is this a wave that I'm purposefully racing toward that will take me out? Or is this yet another wave I can trust the Lord to manage as He allows me to gain His perspective and experience that same problem from the safety of the shore? Remember, He alone speaks to the winds and waves.

HOW WE WAIT TODAY

Relinquishing control of our situations can be challenging. However, when we rush in too quickly, it often causes the circumstance to seem larger than it actually is. Yes, the situation is real, but if we step safely back on the shore of our life, the Lord can give us His perspective of that same situation. There is no moment, event, or trial that is outside of the ability of the Lord to handle. He walks with us and longs for us to relinquish control to Him. How have you worked on trusting the Lord to keep life's waves at arm's length?

DAY 03 | INCREASING OUR FAITH

Thank God! Call out his Name! Tell the whole world who
he is and what he's done! Sing to him! Play songs for him!
Broadcast all his wonders! Revel in his holy Name, God-
seekers, be jubilant! Study God and his strength,
seek his presence day and night;
Remember all the wonders he performed,
the miracles and judgments that came out of his mouth.
—

1 CHRONICLES 16:8-12 (MSG)

We need faith in all shapes and sizes. Sometimes, we need "big faith" for a life decision or healing for a loved one. Sometimes, we ask the Lord to move in a situation, and He does, and our faith is strengthened in our daily lives. Sometimes, faith is exercised, but it looks more like living on the edge, like eating three-day-old sushi. I see you.

Faith, like a muscle, has to be worked to increase. In our everyday lives, that might look like tiny moments of trusting or sighs of surrender. It takes work to build faith and requires remembering to solidify it.

All throughout the Bible, we are reminded to remember. The NIV uses "remember" or "remembered" 231 times from cover to cover.[1] I can only imagine it uses that word so often because we forget.

We forget God's faithfulness. We forget God's character. We forget how much He loves us. We forget He is for us, and with us, and will never leave us.

We need to be better rememberers. Our faith increases as we are reminded of what the Lord has brought us through. It becomes a testimony of how He showed Himself faithful, or how, even when it was terribly difficult, He never left our side. As we recall and recount the story God has written on our hearts, it reinforces to our soul what it has forgotten: He is faithful. He can be trusted.

Faith is simply the distance between God speaking and my willingness to take action on what He said. Sometimes, that way seems easy; sometimes, it seems an impassable chasm. When our faith feels weak, or when we feel threatened or scared, it just means we are focused too much on that space between, instead of choosing to trust that He's already filled the gap and calls us to walk right on across.

Sometimes, faith looks like stepping out and failing. That's hard. It's willingly taking that brave leap but then falling flat on your face. In those moments, it's completely normal to have a thousand questions, to be upset or even angry. However, God is not shocked by those feelings and can shoulder them all. Even when we doubt, God can still show up and write a beautiful ending to the story. Believing "even still" is often more important to our faith journey than taking the first step.

Faith is not dependent on whether things go our way, whether we receive a blessing, or if everything turns out. Instead, faith is crafted in the moments when we don't see the way through—and then, God orchestrates the impossible.

He is not waiting for us to be ready. He's waiting for us to be surrendered.

I also believe He wants us to be mindful of how we talk about our situations in faith. What story will we tell? Will we recount His goodness when we can't see the way through, or will we forget how He's never failed us?

While we're at it, let's thank God for those I-made-it-perspectives. That means we've lived through it and have been given the gift of looking back. It means we're on the other side. We can learn from that experience and increase our faith, lean into that experience, and appreciate all He's done.

I don't know about you, but if I have to experience it, I don't want it to be for nothing. I want to hear from Him, learn, and get to the other side with a story of God's faithfulness, not just a list of how it all went wrong. I want a story I can draw on in the future to remind myself of His faithfulness when I inevitably need to hear it again.

I'm not negating the hard and tragic. It is real, and for our faith to be exercised, often it's necessary to walk that road. I just want God to help me see things from His perspective and allow my faith to grow. I want to remember His goodness and remind myself that while my feelings are unpredictable, His faithfulness never fails.

HOW WE WAIT TODAY

You might be in a season where you feel like your faith is being tested. Is it a time when you sense God asking you to step into the gap and trust that He will be with you, whatever the outcome? Or you might be in a season where you have made the leap, and you're excited to see how God will write this story. Regardless, remember that He is faithful. Remember what He's done in the past and how it can be the assurance that He will be faithful again. He is the same, yesterday, today, and forever.[2] Amen.

(1) Bible Gateway, accessed December 4, 2022, https://www.biblegateway.com/quick-search/?quicksearch=remember&qs_version=NIV.
(2) Hebrews 13:8 (NIV)

DAY 04 | MISSING THE STORM

And he said to them, "Why are you afraid,
O you of little faith?" Then he rose and rebuked the
winds and the sea, and there was a great calm.

—

MATTHEW 8:26 (ESV)

I needed it. Quiet. Solitary. Alone-ness.

As a card-carrying introvert, I have learned that the mechanism the Lord uses to help me refuel is to have me pull back, get alone, and be still. It's where I can get His clarity and enjoy the sweet solace of hearing His voice clearly and revive those parts in me that have worn thin. Recently, I found a pause in a quiet corner of a coffee shop. It had a huge picture window that looked out into the gray afternoon. I read the Word, watched His world, and listened as His voice fed me.

My mind was filled with the here and now: troubles, worries, stresses, what-ifs, the how-do-Is, and the pray-I-get-this-rights. So, I pressed in and read. One verse led to the next, and the passages led me to chapters and books.

Insight. Peace.

I'm not sure when it happened, but I looked out the window and realized everything was dripping. It wasn't raining, though it certainly had been. The storm had come and gone, and I had missed the entire thing.

✦ I was so focused on the Word, hearing the healing, and waiting for the rescue that I missed the storm altogether.

Is that what He intends? Does He wish that we will be so enveloped in Him, seeking Him, and knowing His purposes that the tough times come and go, and we hardly notice?

Does He desire that, after a time of intense eye-locking with Jesus, we look just left of His gaze in amazement to find He's brought us through the storm, barely damp? Does he want us to realize that if we had instead focused on the storm unfolding, we tragically would have memorized every drop, rehearsed every puddle of pain, and recorded every splash?

I think that's exactly what He intends.

Look at the story recorded in three of the Gospels (Luke 8, Matthew

8, Mark 4), where the disciples were caught in a boat during a storm. They were completely freaking out. I picture them wide-eyed, watching the water pour over the sides of the hull, mentally calculating their sure demise. Meanwhile, Jesus is there "in the same boat" with the disciples, experiencing it right alongside them, yet the Prince of Peace was taking a nap. So, outside of telling the storm to chill (as only the Liberating King can), Jesus was essentially missing the entire thing.

His focus was different. Our focus can be different.

We will experience storms in life, no doubt. But keeping our hearts and eyes locked on Him means we'll be watching the only thing that truly matters.

 HOW WE WAIT TODAY

Throughout His Word, the Lord gently reminds us: He is all we need (Matthew 6:33). Keep your heart and eyes focused (Proverbs 4:25). Don't freak out (Prov. 3:5-6). Bad things happen, but it doesn't have to take you down (John 16:33). It's all about where we place our focus. Intentionally lock eyes with the Savior. He will be right there with us, and we will have the beautiful potential to miss the storm altogether.

DAY 05 | SAVORING THE BLESSINGS

May He grant the dreams of your heart and
see your plans through to the end.
When you win, we will not be silent!
We will shout and raise high our banners
in the great name of our God!
May the Eternal say yes to all your requests.

—

PSALM 20:4-5 (VOICE)

In my life, there have been so many moments when I was in such a hurry to get to the next season that I feel sure that I short-changed myself the blessing of the current one. Have you ever felt that way?

The moment came—you did it! Triumph! And then, without really enjoying it at all, moments later, you rub your hands together excitedly, saying, "What's next?"

We need to pause to celebrate the moments and savor the seasons that the Lord has brought us through.

Don't miss it! Take time to reflect on the good He's done. Reflect on what He's brought in and through your life, and the people He used to do it. Celebrate the hard-fought wins. Each part is worth acknowledging, and each holds blessings to be uncovered.

It's equally important to remember that every season doesn't have to be triumphant or victorious for God to use it in a mighty way. As hard as it may be, we should take time to reflect on how He's brought beauty from the ashes and to learn from our failures.

Those times will be the ones we're tempted to rush the most. When it seems we can't leave a season fast enough. It's been hard, and we're ready to move on. If that's where you are, acknowledge the difficulty, thank God for everything He's done in that season—seen and unseen—and ask Him to reveal those blessings to you. Even if it has yet to look like you thought it would or it didn't turn out the way you anticipated it, remember that His ways are higher than ours. His thoughts are higher than our thoughts.[1] There is still much to be learned.

All this reflection takes time, and yes, you guessed it, we must get still and pause to hear His voice. To do that, we must be willing to do the work to get our hearts in a place to truly understand the blessing of that season. Pray, seek, get alone, journal, read, and learn all you can. It's dirt-under-your-nails faith. It's worth it.

And even though we are looking back to be reminded of all He has done, let's also remember the fullness of what's coming! He has more for us![2] He not only wants us to appreciate the current season, but in generosity wants to give us all that we've learned, as a gift to be unwrapped and used for our good in the next.

✛ HOW WE WAIT TODAY

God's faithfulness assures us that we can anticipate the blessings He wants to bring into our lives in the coming season, even as we reflect on the current season or the one we've just left. We can trust that His gifts are good and will be right on time. Fellow Wait-er, let's take our time and savor the changing of each season, not rushing any of them. Take time to pause and hear all He wants to say, celebrate the blessings He has given, and wait with expectation for what will come.

---

(1) Isaiah 55:8–9 (VOICE).
(2) Isaiah 43:19 ibid.

END OF THE WEEK PAUSE

*Where did you sense God's presence this week as you paused to go
SLOW (Stop / Listen / Observe / Wait)?*

What did He teach you as you paused and waited to hear His voice?

What verse made you pause and think this week?

WEEK SIX

WAITING
IN THE WORD

DAY 01 | WHO TOLD YOU THAT?

You are great. You do wonderful things.
You alone are God.
—
PSALM 86:10 (NIRV)

I have a very dear friend who challenges me. (I hope you all have a friend like this in your life.) One day, I sat across from her in her office and poured out all my emotions, words, and thoughts. I used phrases like, "I'm just not great at such and such," and "I won't ever be able to do such and such."

In wisdom and with the open door to my life she knew she had, she looked at me from behind her desk, and said, "Who told you that?" She knew what God's Word said and allowed the Lord to speak through her that day to help heal my heart.

I remember pausing. The hurt was as clear as day. I had bought into a lie. I had just relayed to her what the very real enemy of my soul, Satan, wanted me to believe about myself and that situation. I bought it hook, line, and sinker.

That is how the enemy works. The father of lies, Satan (John 8:44), can only speak in his native tongue—lying. There is no truth in him. He has no new tricks and comes to kill, steal, and destroy our lives (John 10:10). He often does this by getting us to believe lies or even half-truths about who we are and what we can or cannot do.

The Father of truth, our precious loving Jesus (John 14:6), speaks in His native language—truth—because inherently, He is truth and operates only in love. He cannot depart from His nature. Praise God!

You have to know what is being said, to know what to believe. Go to the Source to find out what He is saying about who you are.

As believers, we need to cling to the truth of God's Word. Here are a few truths to get you started:[1]

- **I am a child of God.**

   But for all who did receive and trust in Him, He gave them the right to be reborn as children of God. (John 1:12).

- **I am a friend of Jesus.**

  I don't call you servants any longer; servants don't know what the master is doing, but I have told you everything the Father has said to Me. I call you friends. (John 15:15)

- **My old self was crucified with Christ, and I am no longer a slave to sin.**

  We know this: whatever we used to be with our old sinful ways has been nailed to His cross. So our entire record of sin has been canceled, and we no longer have to bow down to sin's power. (Romans 6:6)

- **I will not be condemned by God.**

  Therefore, now no condemnation awaits those who are living in Jesus the Anointed, the Liberating King. (Romans 8:1)

- **I have been accepted by Christ.**

  So accept one another in the same way the Anointed has accepted you so that God will get the praise He is due. (Romans 15:7)

- **I am a new creature in Christ.**

  Therefore, if anyone is united with the Anointed One, that person is a new creation. The old life is gone—and see—a new life has begun! (2 Corinthians 5:17)

- **I am God's workmanship created to produce good works.**

  For we are the product of His hand, heaven's poetry etched on lives, created in the Anointed, Jesus, to accomplish the good works God arranged long ago. (Ephesians 2:10)

- **The peace of God guards my heart and mind.**

  And know that the peace of God (a peace that is beyond any and all of our human understanding) will stand watch over your hearts and minds in Jesus, the Anointed One. (Philippians 4:7)

- **God supplies all my needs.**

  Know this: my God will also fill every need you have according to His glorious riches in Jesus the Anointed, our Liberating King. (Philippians 4:19)

- **I have been made complete in Christ.**

  You, too, are being completed in Him, the One who has dominion over all rule, all authority. (Colossians 2:10)

These verses represent just a small number of ways God explains the truth about who we are. Remember, God can only speak the truth. When we memorize the Scriptures and allow them to be more than just words (Psalm 119:11), it is like putting a "who told you that" filter in front of our minds and hearts. When we do, we can hold up what we believe next to the truth and the authority of the Scriptures and see how it aligns. If it doesn't, you know you've bought into a lie of the enemy. If that's the case, then it's time to stare him down and say what is true over your life, and let your heart and thoughts align with the loving heart and thoughts of Jesus.

✦ HOW WE WAIT TODAY

What lies are you allowing yourself to believe? What truth in God's Word can you use to combat them? Memorize those Scriptures and stand firm on them, confident that what God says about you is the only truth that matters. Find a version of the Bible you love that you can easily understand, whether online, in an app, or a real paper version, and I promise you'll never regret the time you spend there.

---

(1) These Scripture quotations are from The Voice Bible.

DAY 02 | SELAH

Trust in him at all times, O people;
pour out your heart before him;
God is a refuge for us. Selah

—

PSALM 62:8 (ESV)

The Hebrew word "selah" appears 74 times in the Bible: 71 in the Psalms and 3 in the book of Habakkuk.

Some scholars believe it comes from the word, "calah," which means "to measure" or "weigh in the balances." Another thought is that "selah" is a combination of two Hebrew words: s_lah, "to praise," and s_lal, "to lift up." Still, others believe it derived from salah, "to pause."

And while there is much debate as to the actual meaning of the word, it is, nonetheless, in the Word of God and, therefore, important not to miss.

And that might just be the point.

No matter the definition, the writers used it to gain attention, to pull you aside from the text for a moment, as if to grab you gently by the shoulders and say, "Did you get that? Did you hear what I just said?" They don't want you to miss the moment, this opportunity to wonder at God.

If "selah" combines all of the above, then selah is undoubtedly a reflection of sorts. It's meant to be a moment in time to open your heart and hear God speak.

It might be as fast as the breath a musician takes between one verse and the next. It might be the slightly audible "mmm" and head nod given when a point is made in a sermon that you agree with, or it might even be the purposeful ellipses a writer uses at the end of a thought...

Regardless, take notice. In the Bible, the writer uses "selah" to make sure we are tracking with them—to reflect, to pause in the normal moment and see what God is trying to say.

In Psalm 32:5, the writers use the selah as a point of celebration and wonder.

"I acknowledged my sin to You, And I did not hide my guilt; I said, 'I will confess my wrongdoings to the Lord'; And You forgave the guilt of my sin. Selah." (NASB)

In Psalm 143:6, the writers use the selah when at the end of their rope and in desperation.

"I spread out my hands to You;
My soul longs for You like a thirsty land. Selah." (NKJV)

It was meant to be that inexpressible moment where you are shaking your head at the wonder of the Lord, and words simply won't come. Whether in celebration or sadness, a sense of jumping up and down in your spirit, or sitting with your head in your hands, that's selah. It's a moment to just...be. It's the multi-faceted-yet-one-word term that also best encapsulates *Waiting on Wonders*: Stop. Pause. Reflect. Measure. Praise. Consider. Listen. Watch. Observe. Wait.

Selah.

HOW WE WAIT TODAY

If you've gotten this far in the book, you certainly understand that we can experience God in our everyday moments. All throughout you've seen quotes set aside with the ✦ con to act as a visual reminder to selah and listen to what the Lord might be saying. Today, in your every-day Tuesday kind of moments, consider the selah. As you wait on the wonders the Lord wants to reveal to you, it's okay to not have words or even complete thoughts. Sometimes, all you can do is breathe in pro-foundly and selah. Simply acknowledge His presence as He leads and teaches you in all the ways He is trying to speak to you.

And Joshua said to the people, Sanctify yourselves
[that is, separate yourselves for a special holy purpose],
for tomorrow the Lord will do wonders among you.

—

JOSHUA 3:5 (AMPC)

I want God to use me. I also want to see the Lord do wonders among my friends and those I love. However, sometimes we might be tempted to think we have something to do with the outcome if we don't have our heart in the right place when those things happen. It's our job to be committed to the Lord's honor, not our own. So, setting ourselves apart to honor the Lord with our lives is not only our calling but our responsibility. If we truly want God to work through our lives, we must prepare our hearts to recognize the origin of the wonders. We must be careful to keep our eyes focused on the Maker of the miracle, not the means by which He brought it.

In addition, we must believe in our hearts that He will do wonders among us, that He will show up regardless of how it looks.

Think of the priests in Joshua 3; they probably walked ankle, knee, and maybe even neck deep in the Jordan before they walked on dry land. Don't miss this...

> "When the priests who are carrying the Ark touch the water with their feet, the river will stop flowing as though held back by a dam, and will pile up as though against an invisible wall!" Now it was the harvest season and the Jordan was overflowing all its banks; but as the people set out to cross the river and as the feet of the priests who were carrying the Ark touched the water at the river's edge, *suddenly, far up the river at the city of Adam, near Zarethan, the water began piling up as though against a dam!* And the water below that point flowed on to the Dead Sea until the riverbed was empty. Then all the people crossed at a spot where the river was close to the city of Jericho, and the priests who were carrying the Ark stood on dry ground in the middle of the Jordan and waited as all the people passed by." Joshua 3:13-17 (TLB - emphasis mine)

The river, the text says, was at flood stage. Indeed, the water stopped when the priests' feet touched the water. However, it stopped upstream, not where they were. This means the water was still running with incredible power when they began their walk across, carrying the very presence of the Lord inside the Ark of the Covenant. It didn't stop while they were standing on the bank. It didn't stop until they were in it, and even then, they couldn't see that the Lord was already at work making a way where there was none. But He was.

✦ *He was not only making a way; He was making a wonder.*

Can you imagine how they felt as they got deeper and deeper, and the water yet to slow its torrent and begin its shallowing?

It was when they were in the middle that the miracle came. The middle.

The journey to the middle was undoubtedly slippery, balancing His presence and their faith. Sliding, feet on the unsure ground, pushed on all sides, soaked to the bone. And then, just like that, the ground began to dry. The wall of water that Providence pushed back had arrived. The middle of the walk. The middle of the journey. The middle.

Have you been there? Are you there now? You've committed to setting yourself apart for what He wants, believing all His promises are '"yes" and "amen." Then He asks you to walk into a flood-stage situation with His presence and trust Him that He will make the deluge of whatever the issue is, stop. But will it?

It's sometimes hard to believe He is leading us ultimately to the promised land of all He has for us. Especially when we are looking for a miracle we can't yet see. Yes, I've been there too.

How often have I looked at a flood-stage situation in my life and tiptoed in, complaining that it was too cold, running too fast, the way too messy, or I simply turned away, and said, "no way." How many Jordan-wonders have I missed because I wasn't willing to get neck deep—in the middle—before the Lord revealed how He would rescue? How many times have I whined to Him about how hard it was, when in reality, the flood waters had *already been stopped,* just slightly out of view?

I've been in it, but completely missing it.

I don't want to miss the marvel.

Let's be about the business of the set-apart-life, the one that does things differently and prepares for the wonders He wants to do among us every day.

✦ HOW WE WAIT TODAY

Being set apart means that we choose to be different, set apart in our choices, our actions, and our speech. A set-apart life chooses to follow hard after Christ. That life looks at floods and sees freedom. That life knows journeys don't start easy, but that dry ground comes with a faith that endures. That life shakes off the shackles of flesh and filth and instead runs knee-deep or neck-deep into a torrential flood just to watch the Lord show up. That's the kind of wonder I want to see Him do among us. That's what He's capable of doing in our hearts when we set ourselves apart for Him, when we're willing to go to the middle to experience the miracle.

DAY 04 | GOD'S CLASSROOM

So I brought them out of Egypt and led them into the
wilderness.
—
EZEKIEL 20:10 (NLT)

Several years ago, I had the opportunity to visit Israel and go into the Zin Wilderness. Growing up in America and never having seen the Middle East, I imagined the "wilderness" to be desolate, as depicted in every Moses movie. Yes, there were areas of arid desert, but there were also areas of tropical oasis. There were high treacherous cliffs, impassable mountains, streams, and hidden pools of water.

While in Israel, I learned the wilderness doesn't always look how you think it will, and it's like that in our own lives as well. We don't always recognize when we're entering a lonely, wandering, wilderness season or when we've been sent there to learn something challenging.

Sometimes, it is completely obvious. You see it over the horizon, and you know, yep. It's coming. You steel yourself and walk right into the necessary. Other times, the wilderness arrives at your doorstep. Bam. And you're in. Most often, however, the days of the desert come slowly. You're walking along in life, and one grain of sand at a time, the wilderness takes up residence in your heart. Then, one day you wake up, rub your bone-dry eyes, and realize you're in the middle of a dry and desolate season and don't remember the path that brought you there.

I wonder if the children of Israel felt that way. Even in their complaining, do you think as they wandered the desert, they asked themselves in private moments, "How did we get here...really? How did we get to the place where we were so excited to be liberated, and now we can't stop complaining?"

Had they not seen God be faithful? Had they not experienced His rescue? Had they not lived miracles?

Are they not so different from us?

We are liberated from our own Egypts, and within earshot of the oppression, we are complaining in the desert, wandering in the wilderness, unaware of how the journey unfolded. We find ourselves trying to be the provider, trying to fix all the things, instead of relying on the one who brought us there.

✦ *Be very clear. He hasn't left us there. He's leading us there.*

My friend, Marc Turnage, says the wilderness is God's classroom.[1]

There is always discipline in the dust.

The Hebrew name for the book of Numbers is "in the wilderness." It is full of specifics of how things should be ordered and life should happen. It's also a story of how things go awry. But, ultimately, it's also a tale of you and me. Numbers is an aptly named account of the history that still camps out in our veins, the discounted details, and the slow drift. Over and over.

However, the thing to remember is that the Lord provided a way out. And the same will be true for us. No matter how long we've been wandering, no matter how much complaining we've done, and the ways we've forgotten His faithfulness, He will split the Jordan of our circumstances to bring us into the promised land of all He has for us. It's the wonder of the wilderness.

✦ **HOW WE WAIT TODAY**

Wilderness seasons are meant to teach us, so I try not to despise the dry-desert times. God guides us—sometimes quite abruptly—sometimes very slowly, but always for our own good. And although it seems dry in the waiting, there is an oasis and a way out—every time. It's a beautiful gift to be able to walk with the Lord in the dry times. As we do, we'll gather the dust of that experience on our feet all along the journey. Then, we can take what we've learned, and walk with that knowledge right up to the high places of flourishing. The dust we carry on our feet will help us remember the journey. It will be a monument to the moment He took us in...and when He brought us out.

---

(1) Turnage, Marc, *Windows into the Bible: Cultural and Historical Insights from the Bible for Modern Readers* (Springfield, Missouri: Logion Press, 2016), 31.

DAY 05 | MUSICAL MOMENTS

Make a joyful noise unto the Lord, all the earth: make a
loud noise, and rejoice, and sing praise.

—

PSALM 98:4 (KJV)

Sometimes, people will ask, "Hey T, what's your favorite song?" or "What are you listening to these days?" For a worship pastor, this is a natural question. So, I usually rattle off the name of the most recent song that has wrecked my heart or a lyric the Lord has used to undo me in my personal times of worship.

Music and lyrics are powerful. They can immediately transport you to another time and wrap you up in all the feelings of the moment. Music is useful. Throughout the Bible, it is used for worship, to cause the singer and listener to recall God's faithfulness, to express lament and grief, celebration, and joy. It was created to give God back the breath He put in our lungs. Music is meant for the largest of triumphs and the smallest of ordinary moments. It applies just as much in large gatherings as in private whispers. It transcends age, race, culture, and time.

We will undoubtedly have favorite songs. Maybe they are tied to an epic moment or a breakthrough in a particular season. However, over the years, I've decided I really do have a unique set of favorite songs. They are not love songs that take me back to the '90s or Christmas carols that remind me of memories we've made. These songs aren't on the Top 40 list or the latest worship releases. They are entirely different kinds of God-created sounds.

My favorite songs are the sounds of my boys, my Sons of Thunder, playing soccer in the kitchen, complete with commentary and crowd noise. It's the sound of my youngest's hysterical laughter, when he's watching his friend's latest gaming hilarity, and he laughs so hard he can hardly breathe. It's the echo of my boys wrestling upstairs so loudly that I begin to pray for the integrity of the ceiling. It's the rumble of my husband's truck pulling in the driveway, the constant hum of the dishwasher and the clang of coins in the dryer. The sound of the refrigerator door opening at midnight. It's prayers whispered over those same boys at night before bed, and stories told at dinner.

Sometimes, the best songs aren't found on a playlist; they are heard in the heart.

I hear songs with unlikely lyrics: "Get your shoes on," "Can I please have more," "Are you sure you brushed your teeth," and "Don't touch your brother." These melodies are precious pauses etched in my soul like those that get stuck in your head. But these are songs I *don't* want to forget. When I'm 80, I want to remember every line and lyric. I'm so glad I get to sing along to these songs that sound like the sweet presence of Jesus, singing right back to me. They don't rhyme, are not necessarily catchy, and break all the rules I've learned about proper songwriting. Still, they are so good that I'm learning to quiet the rest of my life so I can tune in when they start. Spotify wouldn't stream them, and Apple Music wouldn't promote them, but I'm attaching memories to each melody and learning to memorize every word.

✦ **This is the music of the mundane and it is a melody worth memorizing.**

God is helping me hear His voice in these unconventional songs and is giving me a fresh perspective on what happens when I stop to listen. These familiar songs are a sort of everyday worship. I'm learning to pause with each line and lyric, as He lovingly writes the soundtrack of my life.

✦ **HOW WE WAIT TODAY**

What songs do you hear around your house? What beautiful songs are being sung in your life but might be disguised as the messy and ordinary? Any moment can be a holy one. Fellow Wait-er, let's retune our hearts to recognize the beauty in even the normal "songs" of life.

END OF THE WEEK PAUSE

Where did you sense God's presence this week as you paused to go SLOW (Stop / Listen / Observe / Wait)?

What did He teach you as you paused and waited to hear His voice?

What verse made you pause and think this week?

WHEN THE WAITING IS HARD

DAY 01 | WHEN YOU'RE SEARCHING

I love those who love me;
those who search hard for me will find me.

—

PROVERBS 8:17 (VOICE)

Have you ever been looking for something you thought, for sure, you would find? A job? A house? A car? An avocado that is just right? (Why is that so hard?)

Or maybe something much more significant.

A word from the Lord? A healing touch? A desire to be truly known?

There have been many times when I have been searching—searching for an answer when the way seems dark. Searching for healing for a friend when it's taking way too long. Searching to hear His voice when He seems to be silent. Searching for significance in a world that always leaves you wanting. Searching for purpose in a way too busy life.

Asking all the hard questions. Getting none of the answers.

Just being real. Have you ever been there? You are not alone.

As humans, we are seekers. We are on an eternal quest to find what our souls are looking for. We do a great job of trying to fill up voids in our lives with every other thing, except what will completely satisfy us—the love and grace of Jesus. We need to be refilled daily by the Holy Spirit to receive His power to live the abundant life God set out for us to live.

When we find ourselves searching, it is an alert that we're trying to refill our lives with things other than the Father.

Instead of seeking things as answers to our questions, we need to turn to God, who is ready to refill us and ultimately be everything we've been after all along. We all need to be refilled. We all have a choice as to what we try to refill our lives with. (Spoiler alert: there is only One thing that actually satisfies—and it's not the thing we're worried about.) It's all about searching for the right thing.

Recently, I was walking along a beach, thinking, praying, and asking some hard questions. I needed to hear from the Lord. As I walked along, I was reminded that I was on a stretch of beach known for a particularly rare and valuable shell found only in a few locations in the world. Within minutes, my walk soon turned from "I need to talk to the Lord and get some clarity on some things," to "I need to find this shell." My focus shifted, and I became obsessed with unearthing this shell. (Mind you, I'd walked that beach over the last 20+ years more times than I could count and had never found one. Not one). But there I was, bent over, carefully scanning the sand and turning over any shell I saw, picking some up and dusting them off. I had been on this quest for about 30 minutes, ankle-deep in the water, when the Lord stopped me in my tracks.

The pause.

He said, "What do you think would happen if you were seeking me as hard as you are looking for this shell? What if you were picking up and turning every thought over to me? If you were dusting off your doubt and handing it to me to examine? If you were standing ankle-deep in my presence, watching me turn it all for good?"

Needless to say, I stopped shell searching that day. It was just a tiny moment on the beach where I paused to hear His voice and He gave me clarity in that moment. He alone is what refuels and fills us. If you feel like you're searching, put all of that same effort and energy into searching for Him. There will never be a greater prize.

✧ HOW WE WAIT TODAY

Are you searching? If so, let that searching be a gentle reminder to seek the only One who can fill you. Put your focus on the One who can make you whole, and who alone, holds the answers. Seek Him with your whole heart. Only He can satisfy.

Eternal One: Leave this cave,
and go stand on the mountainside in My presence.

The Eternal passed by him. The mighty wind separated
the mountains and crumbled every stone before the
Eternal. This was not a divine wind, for the Eternal was
not within this wind. After the wind passed through,
an earthquake shook the earth. This was not a divine
quake, for the Eternal was not within this earthquake.
After the earthquake was over, there was a fire. This was
not a divine fire, for the Eternal was not within this fire.

After the fire died out, there was nothing but the sound
of a calm breeze. And through this breeze a gentle,
quiet voice entered into Elijah's ears. He covered his
face with his cloak and went to the mouth of the cave.
Suddenly, Elijah was surprised.

Eternal One: Why are you here, Elijah?
What is it that you desire?

—

1 KINGS 19:11-13 (VOICE)

When all hell is breaking loose, what do you listen for?

You feel alone. The avalanche of life is threatening to turn your world to rubble. The roar of life's deafening winds nearly knocks you off your feet. Your world is shaking. What once was a steady place is now no longer. The heat of all that consumes you is scorching your soul. It's a mess.

When chaos comes, conversations with the Lord tend to be cut-and-dried:

Where are you?

Why are you doing this to us?

Are you even listening?

Do you care what's happening to me?

Honest questions.

None the Lord can't handle.

All He wants to lovingly address within the safety of His presence.

Sometimes, calamity will get our attention and jolt us into a recognition of His presence. While He doesn't cause the chaos, He certainly can use anything to speak to us.

And sometimes, calamity is simply just noise. We glorify the wind, quake, and fire and foolishly show contempt for the simplicity of the peace He brings—as if that alone isn't enough.

When the world is falling apart, it's easier to focus on it crashing down around us than being willing to wait to hear His voice. However, this is possibly the most significant pause we can make. When the final echo of the pandemonium ceases, there *will* be a voice. That whisper will be the one that will give us the strength to continue. That quiet voice will gently speak. That voice will say to our hearts, "Precious one, why are you here? What is it that you desire?"

When it's all coming down, don't be so consumed with the wind and quake and fire that you miss His voice in the middle of it.

He is with you. He is speaking.

HOW WE WAIT TODAY

While it's easy to do, be mindful not to embrace the misfortune and be courted by the wind, quake, and fire. Instead, listen for His still, small voice. It will be the bedrock in the middle of the mess. It will be your solid ground to stand on when all else is caving in. He can be trusted to be your Prince of Peace today.

DAY 03 | HIS TIMING, NOT OURS

*Don't be impatient. Wait for the Lord, and he will come
and save you! Be brave, stouthearted, and courageous.
Yes, wait and he will help you.*

—

PSALM 27:14 (TLB)

S ome of you are on top of the world. Your family is great, your ministry is thriving, your friendships are fruitful, and your team is winning. Some of you are in a season of literal waiting—waiting for a phone call, restoration, healing, or the next step. Some of you are between seasons—moving from the bounty of spring and summer into the hard work of fall and winter. Some of you are just returning from vacation, while some have been hand-to-the-plow for months.

All that to say, let's pretend we're at a coffee shop and we've just sat down together. Imagine me looking you in the eyes, and saying this. "Whether you've been in this pursuit of Jesus for 3 weeks or 103 years, wait for it. Whatever God has for you will happen; just know that it will take time to become a reality. Be patient, and don't give up ahead of seeing it come full circle".

Recently, I saw that quote, "The day you plant the seed is not the day you eat the fruit."[1] Right? This is true in your family, marriage, job, kids, and relationships.

✦ *We have to be willing to wait on the fruition of God's faithfulness and patiently wait for Him to complete the good work He has started. The seeds of faithfulness sown in the soil of time and watered with a deluge of patience will yield the fruit of favor and blessing—if we wait for it.*

Yes. Jesus can do things instantly. However, remember even the things that were done in an instant in Jesus' ministry were steeped in 30 years of growing, learning, humbling Himself, and keeping Himself pressed to the Father.

From the outside, it looked like Jesus' ministry was happening "all of the sudden," but a lot of waiting had elapsed before it was His time to begin.

Sometimes, people we love want it to be our season or the time to be right before it is. All with good intentions, all in love—but don't let someone else's excitement for you be your compass. The only timeline that matters is the Father's.

We can beg a flower to bloom, but until it hears the voice of its Creator saying it's the time, it won't happen. Likewise, no matter what we hope will happen or even try to fabricate, nothing can stop the plans the Lord has for us.[2] Stay open to the Creator's voice and stay pressed into Him to know when the season has arrived for the next beautiful thing to unfold. His timing is perfect.

HOW WE WAIT TODAY

As you are waiting, learn all you can. If you're excited about your next season, but hear the Lord say, "wait for it," be encouraged that you're not alone, and find others who can walk with you in the waiting. If you are in that season of anticipation, keep pressed to the Father's heart and know full well that when the voice of your Creator says it's time, nothing can stop it.

(1) Fabienne Fredrickson, Goodreads, accessed November 12, 2022, https://www.goodreads.com/author/quotes/6938684.Fabienne_Fredrickson.
(2) Job 42:2 (ESV).

DAY 04 | OBEDIENCE

If you listen obediently to the Voice of God,
your God, and heartily obey all his commandments
that I command you today, God, your God, will place
you on high, high above all the nations of the world.
All these blessings will come down on you and spread
out beyond you because you have responded
to the Voice of God, your God:
God's blessing inside the city,
God's blessing in the country;
God's blessing on your children,
the crops of your land, the young of your livestock,
the calves of your herds,
the lambs of your flocks.
God's blessing on your basket and bread bowl;
God's blessing in your coming in,
God's blessing in your going out.

—

DEUTERONOMY 28:1 (MSG)

Obedience is hard. It's choosing to do what you know to be right even though you might not want to. Although I'm a relatively disciplined person, I sometimes don't want to do the necessary things to create a disciplined life. Would you agree it's much easier (and satisfying), to eat a piece of cake than to get in the car, head to the gym, and sweat that cake off? Um, Yes. However, I know when I do, I feel better and see the kind of results I'm after. But it's hard. And it takes intentionality.

Spiritual obedience is hard. Doing the right thing and choosing to obey the Lord can be difficult and might even seem like it doesn't make sense. To complicate matters, Satan is happy to keep us distracted and usually offers an easy exit just before the best parts of obedience are realized! It's easy not to do the right thing.

There have been plenty of times when I've been faced with the option to obey what I know to be true or what I feel God is asking me to do—or cut and run—and I've chosen the latter. However, walking in obedience with the Lord and giving Him our "yes," even in the very normal things, always leads to a far greater payoff if we're willing to trust Him and obey.

I grew up attending a small Methodist church just outside of Atlanta. I learned to love the Lord in that church, and even as a child sitting in the wooden pews, I began to memorize the truth of God's Word through singing hymns. While these aren't sung as much in modern worship environments today, I still hear the timeless lyrics of hymns in my ears when I think of trusting Jesus, following after Him, and choosing to obey.

Jesus, Jesus, how I trust Him!

How I've proved Him o'er and o'er

Jesus, Jesus, precious Jesus!

Oh, for grace to trust Him more[1]

✛ **Obeying the Lord shows that we love Him and put His desires first in our lives. I've found that if this feels conventional, it's probably not sacrificial. And even though it's more challenging, I'd rather be found on the backside of sacrificial obedience walking in a blessing that He's poured out for me, than in mere compliance that comes with ease.**

The best part of sacrificial obedience is that when the blessings come from making the hard choice, that's not the end! It's only the beginning, as I am allowed to steward that blessing He gives and fully walk out the incredible plan He has for me.

Obedience is actually a gift to me from the Father! With the right attitude, what comes to me, if allowed to be worked out fully in me, is ultimately for me. What a precious Jesus. Oh, for grace to trust Him more.

✛ **HOW WE WAIT TODAY**

Obedience is tricky. There is rarely a medal given for making the right choice. However, choosing to focus on what we know to be the proper decision means, in the end, we win Him! Jesus is the prize. There is no greater reward than knowing our lives are honoring Him! So today, as you pause in moments when you are tempted to choose the easy way, instead of the excellent way, remember the blessing that will come from a good choice and hard obedience. What we do with what God gives us today will determine the depth of what He can do through us tomorrow. May we be found joyfully walking in full obedience to our King.

---

(1) Stead, Louisa M.R., *Songs of Triumph*, "'Tis So Sweet to Trust in Jesus," 1882.

DAY 05 | SPIRITUALLY DRY

O God, you are my God; earnestly I seek you; my soul thirsts for you; my flesh faints for you, as in a dry and weary land where there is no water.

—

PSALM 63:1 (ESV)

There are times when we feel on top of the world: our prayer life is exciting, the Word is leaping off the pages, and we're operating in our giftings and feeling alive. We're pausing to hear the Lord—and He speaks! We feel encouraged and are able to encourage others. We are memorizing Scripture, and the Lord brings it to mind for just the right person or situation.

And then, there are those times when heaven is silent. You read the Bible, and you are either confused or bored and can't figure out where the Lord is. You are walking through your daily disciplines of prayer, and Bible study that used to bring life, and yet it feels like you've entered a one-way relationship, and you're feeling empty.

All of these feelings can lead to a sense of complacency in our relationship with the Lord. And whether from our own doing or from entering a time of quiet and mystery from the Lord, the good news is He has not left us, and doesn't love us any less. Whatever your situation, it can be a gentle reminder to persevere and find the Lord in everyday moments, even when you struggle to see Him.

Although the Lord desires a relationship with us on an ongoing basis, His heart for us doesn't change even in times when we're "not feeling it." That's the time we should press in all the more.

We have to learn to persevere through our feelings, which are fickle and will lie to us. Instead, choosing faith, we need to focus on what is true about God and to see our circumstances as tools to build the steel in our souls and help us survive hard seasons.

When I'm feeling spiritually dry because I've let my fire for Him go cold, I have to do the daily disciplines that will keep that flame lit. I also have to give myself enough grace to not be perfect and then accept the grace He so freely gives that gently draws me back to Him. I need to remember that it's more important to get on with the business of being more like Him than focusing on the days when I am not.

If I'm feeling like I'm walking through a dry time because I'm desperate for a word from Him—any word—and it seems He's not responding, I have to remember He is always speaking to me. It just might not sound like what I think it does. Perhaps I just need to retune my attention and recognize it could be found in the next normal moment—feeling the wind on my face, while walking the dog, or folding the laundry. He is in it all.

If this 40-day journey has taught us anything, it's that we are only one normal moment away from hearing His voice and experiencing His presence.

✦ HOW WE WAIT TODAY

Our responsibility is to tend to the fire of our soul and the way we do that is to stay close to the source of the flame. We must keep close proximity to the Light of the World in order to be in line with His will, hear His heart, and be able to discern His leading. However, when you are feeling spiritually dry, realize that He is ever-waiting and wanting to be with you. Fellow Wait-er, if you are in that place...pause. Because a heart at rest, hears. He can't wait to be with you again.

END OF THE WEEK PAUSE

Where did you sense God's presence this week as you paused to go SLOW (Stop / Listen / Observe / Wait)?

What did He teach you as you paused and waited to hear His voice?

What verse made you pause and think this week?

PRACTICAL PAUSES

DAY 01 | JOY VS. HAPPINESS

*You will show me the way of life, granting me the
joy of your presence and the pleasures of living with
you forever.*

—

PSALM 16:11 (NLT)

Are you happy?

Recently, I was talking with a young friend about the difference between joy and happiness. We were discussing what a difference it makes to chase true, deep, abiding joy in our lives instead of settling for temporary happiness. Out of that conversation, I decided to study what the Bible has to say about these similar, yet very different words.

> Joy is a fruit of the spirit or something that develops from a spirit-filled life.[1] Happiness is good and simply the fruit of a good moment.

> Joy takes time to develop and grow. It happens over time and has staying power. Happiness can pop up out of nowhere and disappear just as fast. (Think of the most recent video you watched that made you laugh or smile, and then you forgot 10 minutes later).

> Joy is a product of patience and being willing to wait for the best, not just the easy. Happiness is a product of the quick fix, the fastest answer, and the shortest route.

There isn't anything wrong with happiness and I would say the Father wants you to be happy, but more than that, He wants you to experience true JOY, and they are very different.

True joy takes time. It's longstanding and a result of letting God do a deep work over the course of your life. To borrow the title from Eugene Peterson's book[2], it's the product of "long obedience in the same direction." When we see God working in our lives over our lifetime, that's when the heart begins to develop not just happiness, but joy.

Faith in God is a slow, patient, lifelong work. There is no shortcut to a deep faith in God. He is completely and always easily accessible, but walking with the Lord day-by-day is what helps develop the deep joy that sustains, not the surface happiness that is here today, gone tomorrow.

✦ **The problem is we often want the fruit of joy but not the path it takes to get there.**

We will settle for happiness because it's faster, even though it's less fulfilling. It's not fruit; it's just fast food. Happiness is a fleeting feeling and will pass.

Joy is a connectedness to the heart of the Father that comes from knowing Him, learning more about Him, and knowing, above all, He has good plans for you.[3] Let's not settle for happiness when joy is available to us. And in His presence there is fullness of joy. Pause in His presence today and experience what He offers there. That is the joy we're after.

✦ HOW WE WAIT TODAY

When we think about happiness, oftentimes, we think about not being happy. Yes, there are times and seasons when we will not have feelings of happiness. This is very real. However, the undercurrent of true joy can carry us even when our feelings leave us high and dry. If you are struggling to find joy, be sure to share that with a trusted friend, pastor, or family member. God wants you to get the help you need and can use other people and resources to accomplish that great work. I have benefitted from professional counseling in seasons where I struggled with finding joy and would recommend it to all! The Lord longs for you to experience the true abiding joy that comes from being in His presence. Ask Him to show you joy, not just happiness, as you seek Him and learn to hear His voice.

(1) Galatians 5.22 (NLT).
(2) Peterson, Eugene H., A Long Obedience in the Same Direction: Discipleship in an Instant Society (Westmont, IL: InterVarsity Press, 2000), 3.
(3) Jeremiah 29:11 (NLT).

DAY 02 | GRATITUDE

Enter his gates with thanksgiving and his courts with
praise; give thanks to him and praise his name.

—

PSALM 100:4 (NIV)

When my children were small, we memorized Psalm 100 as a family. It was very cute to listen to a two-year-old saying "give fanks to Him and pwaise His name" and mispronounce most of the words. In the process of having them memorize it, my husband and I memorized it too. It is now one of my favorite passages in the Bible, and I particularly love verse 4 that encourages us to give thanks and praise.

It is an encouragement to me to be thankful for things I love; my family, my church, my friends. It's also a reminder to be thankful for things I don't as easily say "thank you" for: trials I don't want to face and moments when I have no idea what to do.

The Bible calls this a sacrifice of praise. It hurts to give it—and it's costly. But it's that kind of thank you that unlocks God's presence in an incredible way.

It's a thank you of surrender, a thank you of remembering God's faithfulness in the past, even though you can't yet trace His hand today.

In The Message version, Psalm 100 reads,

> *Enter with the password: "Thank you!" Make yourselves*
> *at home, talking praise. Thank Him. Worship Him.*

No matter your circumstance, the password to His presence is "Thank You."

Today, I'm thinking about that harder kind of thankfulness, when life has been, well, extra.

In my experience, shifting our perspective, even for a moment, on the small things helps me to assess the larger, more painful things with a different kind of gratitude. So, I'm hoping to spin thankfulness on its head and shift the perspective on what it means to be thankful.

I'm thankful for:

> Laundry that doesn't stop: because it means that my family has clothes to wear, no matter how smelly.

Dishes that pile up and take on a life of their own: because it means that my family has food to eat.

Bills that come out of nowhere: because it means that we have an opportunity to see God show up, even when the numbers don't make sense.

Making beds and changing sheets (and learning to fold the fitted ones): because it means we have a warm, soft place to rest at night.

A slightly dented-in garage door that makes the worst noise you've ever heard: because when it goes up, it means my husband is about to walk through the door.

The years of picking up toys: because it means I have two boys who have brought me more joy than I could ever express. (And because I don't get to do it anymore, I really do miss it.)

These are things I can grumble about and miss the opportunity to be thankful for, *or* they can be daily reminders of God's presence, goodness, and faithfulness in my life in so many ways.

HOW WE WAIT TODAY

Gratitude starts with a "thank you." We might be in a season where we sense the Lord's favor and blessing, or we might be in the most challenging year of our lives. Regardless, let's be grateful people, as we remember God is still worthy of all praise and thanks in everything. Staying grateful is the key to His presence. What can you say "thank you" for today?

*Then Jacob awoke from his sleep and said, "Surely the
Lord is in this place, and I wasn't even aware of it!"*

—

GENESIS 28:16 (NLT)

Have you ever been watching a movie or reading a book and had "that moment"? It's when the character starts the final monologue, or you turn the page toward the end of the book, and you have that "aha," where the pieces just seem to fall together. Maybe that moment makes you stop and look wide-eyed at the person next to you in the theater as you stare in disbelief at what you've heard. Maybe you slowly close your book in joyful astonishment and stare into space, blinking, to take it all in for a few moments. Every good story has that moment. It's a moment where the writer crafts an ending so magical and mysterious that you could never have seen it coming. However, if you watch the movie again or read the book one more time, you can see it as clear as day.

The story in Genesis 28 is like that well-crafted moment. Jacob was on the run from his brother Esau and, on his journey toward Haran, needed to rest. So, he laid down in a field with a stone for a pillow, and the Lord gave him the most incredible dream. He dreamt of a ladder, with the top reaching toward Heaven and angels ascending and descending on it. At the very top was the Lord, who began speaking to Jacob. He told him that not only was He promising the land where he was resting his head would be his inheritance, but that his descendants would be as many as specks of dust. God promised His presence would be with him. And then Jacob woke up.

Can you imagine? This was Jacob's first encounter with God. The first words out of his mouth when he woke up were, "Surely the Lord is in this place, and I wasn't even aware of it!" He recognized God's presence and then had an incredible realization. He understood that not only was God was with him and speaking to him, but that the place where he was, suddenly became a *holy place*. A place to meet with God.

I remember having those first encounters with God in everyday moments. It was as if the monologue had just ended, the page had turned in my spirit, and I realized God was *with* me. Not just on the weekend at church. Not just as I read my Bible. He was there with me in that kindergarten hallway, as I looked at my beloved plumeria trees, and as I did the dishes. Surely, the Lord was in that place—*and I wasn't even aware of it*. He had been with me all along, and I had been missing it! He had made that hallway holy. He had made that moment in my yard with the plumeria tree, a monument of His presence. Every dish I washed was an opportunity to hear Him speak.

✦ *Every moment could be a holy one. A place to meet with God.*

We've been on a journey together for the last eight weeks to discover God's presence in our everyday moments. I hope that as we've walked and wondered together, you've been able to see the Lord a bit more clearly and recognize His presence, even in unlikely places. Every moment, we're given a chance to wait on the wonders He wants to reveal to us.

✦ **HOW WE WAIT TODAY**

You will likely not be on the run from your brother and need to find a place to rest in a rocky field in order to hear from the Lord. However, like Jacob, I know you can experience God's presence wherever you are, no matter the circumstance. I pray that you are more and more aware that He is speaking, and you are pausing long enough to hear what He is saying. As you hear Him speak to you today, remember that any moment can be a holy one. A place to meet with God.

DAY 04 | PATIENCE

May we never tire of doing what is good and right before our Lord because in His season we shall bring in a great harvest if we can just persist.

—

GALATIANS 6:9 (VOICE)

Waiting makes us stop in some way. It can be that pause I try to take before answering too quickly, or the breath I take after saying something hurtful, and I know I need to apologize. It is an interruption in life that has the power to cause change if we let it. In this book, I've worked to capture some of the small-ish moments where I feel like God is purposefully interrupting my busy life so that I can see Him and hear Him more clearly. That's what *Waiting on Wonders* is all about.

Today's pause to consider is, "How are we letting times of waiting refine us?"

We can either see these pauses in our lives as debilitating distractions, and we can be characterized by frustration, impatience, and anger, or we can see them as inspired intersections.

These times of waiting are where the Lord just wants to take our face in His loving hands for a moment and say, "Hey, I love you. Let me show you how much in this little interruption."

Remember, He's always speaking. We just have to slow down our lives long enough to actually hear what He is saying.

In the midst of all this talk about waiting and pausing and learning, here's what I've realized recently: I don't wait well. However, suppose I worked on training my eyes to see Jesus, ears to hear Him, and heart to recognize His voice in tiny moments of waiting. If I did, by practicing His presence in this way, when it really counted, I'd be able to recognize His voice more quickly when I need to hear Him in a significant way in the larger moments.

I'm learning, ever so slowly, how to let times of waiting change me. I am learning to willingly slow down and listen for what He wants to say in the ordinary moments in the inevitable anticipation of the times when I know waiting will come.

Sometimes when we see someone's highlight reel, we want the end product, not what it took to get there. It took time and preparation.

In addition, we have to be careful not to look at the season other people are in, thinking they have gotten where they are without sacrifice and time. Their journey is unique to them and has no bearing on our journeys.

Waiting can be hard. It can test our patience and feel like a personal assault on our agenda. But, if everything in our life is there for a reason and ultimately can purposefully draw us closer to Jesus, we're left with a decision. How do we face these waiting moments and see them not as obstacles but as opportunities? How will I allow this waiting to do its work in me?

✦ HOW WE WAIT TODAY

Be encouraged that there has never been one waiting moment, large or small, whether at the grocery store or carpool line, career change or doctor's office, personal trial, airport, or just a seemingly insignificant moment in your kitchen that the Lord hasn't been right. there. with. you. Be watching for Him. He loves for us to discover Him in the moments we least expect to see Him. He's with us in the waiting.

DAY 05 | SABBATH

Thus God blessed day seven and made it special—an
open time for pause and restoration, a sacred zone of
Sabbath-keeping, because God rested from all the work
He had done in creation that day.

—

GENESIS 2:3 (VOICE)

One of my favorite things I've learned in the last several years is how to rest.[1]

As a serial over-worker, I shamefully prided myself for years on working past hours, seven days a week, and burning the candle at both ends. These lifestyle choices landed me a variety of health issues for many years and, at its height, critical mental and emotional burnout. My body forced me to rest. In doing so, I learned what true rest, a true sabbath, was all about.

Looking back, while the choices were mine, and I take responsibility for allowing my life to make the turns it did, I know that I would have been able to handle the weight of what I was carrying in a healthier way, had I better instituted the discipline of Sabbath.

While I grew up in church and knew about the Sabbath, it had not made its way into my heart and weekly routine. For all of my adult life, I had treated the Sabbath like another day off—a day to run errands and get the rest of the lists done. It wasn't until I studied and learned more about it, that I realized there was so much more that the Lord had for me in this day of rest.

The Sabbath is the fourth commandment in Exodus 20:8 and the only one that starts with "remember." I believe, because we forget.

"Remember the Sabbath day, to keep it holy." (ESV)

Keeping a day holy means setting it apart, making it special and different. In the Old Testament, we see ways this commandment was made overly legalistic. Jesus, who came to set us all free, healed, and did things on the Sabbath, and got in a lot of trouble with the Pharisees for doing so. However, He made it clear that the Sabbath was for man, not man for the Sabbath.[2] And while it's not directly mentioned in the New Testament as a commandment, things that are good for us don't have to be commands for us to benefit from them.

Sabbath is meant to be a day to rest—rest from work, striving, hustling, getting it all done, and worrying about those things.[3] When we enter into purposeful rest, especially in hectic seasons, we are more likely to be equipped to respond well to our spouses, children, and friends, instead of reacting in frustration, sarcasm, negativity, or downright anger.

Sabbath comes from the word "Shabbat" in Hebrew, which means "to stop, rest, delight." Everything we do, or don't do, on that day should be run through that filter. The other six days of the week are capable of holding everything else. When I trust the Lord with my Sabbath day and intentionally stop, rest, and delight in Him, He miraculously multiplies the time in the rest of my week. He gives me space to do more than I thought possible.

Are there weeks when I arrive at the Sabbath with piles of laundry, responsibilities, and undone to-dos? And as a planner and "do-er," does it make me crazy? Absolutely. But there is beauty in laying those things aside for one day, trusting the Lord with those hours, and realigning my heart with His.

Every seven days, I'm given the opportunity to show how much I trust the Lord, not only with my heart—but with my calendar.

The Sabbath is for us. It is a day when we are able to respond to the presence of Jesus, enjoy what delights His heart, and retune our ears to hear His voice. It is a gift waiting to be unwrapped 52 times a year.

HOW WE WAIT TODAY

Depending on your line of work, Sunday might not be the best day for you to take a day of rest. Regardless, choose a day, put it on your calendar, and set it apart to spend time with the Lord. If you have young children in the house, go into Sabbath-keeping knowing that it will look different in each season. Invite them into the rhythms of rest on the Sabbath. Start where you are and know the Lord honors your heart to set apart the day and doesn't want you to bow to any legalism. Remember, fellow Wait-er; this is *for* you, not something He wants *from* you.

---

(1) John Mark Comer's research in this area has been very impactful to me. I highly recommend his books, especially *Garden City* and *The Ruthless Elimination of Hurry.*
(2) Then he said to them, "The Sabbath was made for man, not man for the Sabbath." Mark 2:27 (NIV).
(3) These verses have helped me learn how to take a Sabbath from: striving (Psalm 46:10); worry (Matthew 6:25-33); getting it all done (Matthew 6:34); and worrying about those things (Philippians 4:6).

END OF THE WEEK PAUSE

Where did you sense God's presence this week as you paused to go SLOW (Stop / Listen / Observe / Wait)?

What did He teach you as you paused and waited to hear His voice?

What verse made you pause and think this week?

FOREHEAD TO THE FLOOR

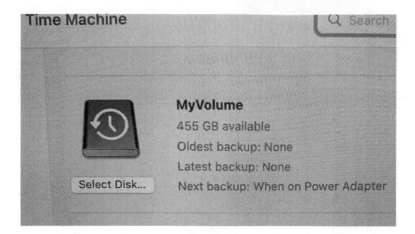

"Tara, I'm sorry. If it's been deleted from the cloud, not just your computer, there is absolutely nothing that can be done to get it back."

And with those words from the Apple Genius, my body began to shake. Tears and uncontrollable sobs were my only response. All the blood rushed from my face. I was sure I was about to pass out.

My entire writing library—every blog post draft waiting to post, a 6-week worship curriculum I'd written, transcripts from speaking engagements, copious notes on "things you should write about," dozens of voice memos and meticulous notes from sermons and podcasts, and most painfully, what would eventually become the book's introduction and all my files of ideas for the devotional entries I would develop, gone. Over 12 years of work compiled, organized, and tagged in a folder—in one moment—gone.

394 files.

In a motion with a mouse that I had done thousands of times, I accidentally swept that folder on my desktop, which was being synced to the cloud, into the trash—and emptied it. I was one week from launching a book-writing journey, and it was all gone.

As soon as the trash made the emptying sound, I grabbed my throat. Wait. Hold up. Where's my writing folder? Search bar: "waiting on wonders."

Zero results. Okay, don't panic. What else was in there? My mind was racing. Search bar: "worship curriculum." Zero results.

All I could say as I began to cry was, "Oh no, oh no, oh no. Jesus, bring it back! Please bring it back!" I slammed my hands on my desk and cry-screamed to my husband, who just happened to walk in at that moment. "I don't want to have to write about this!!" in a knowing sort of way that the Lord would want me to and sensing that He was getting ready to walk right into the sadness with me.

More panic set in. I wildly searched my computer in all the normal places, undoing, attempting to restore, looking for documents, desperate. I got on the phone with Apple, and they walked me through steps I had already tried, transferred me to someone else who attempted two more things I'd already tried, and then, with a long pause, said, "Tara. I'm sorry."

Now, fellow Wait-er, before you come at me with "backup files" and "data recovery software" and every wagging finger in my face, you need to understand that this folder was in the cloud, happily backed up to all devices safely, and had been for many years. I had a brand-new computer and in the set up process, I had not yet turned on the magic of Time Machine to double protect my files like on my previous computer (which, for you PC users out there, Time Machine is Apple's onboard backup system, and a critical detail in this story). What you also need to know is what happened was not irresponsible; it was a freak accident. That writing folder, which was safely synced to the cloud from my desktop, got hidden behind a huge pile of images I was editing. When the unused images got put in the trash from the desktop, so did the folder.

For two hours, I cried. I scoured the internet for some tech wizardry that would undo what I had done. Everything I read was either things I had tried or flatly conveyed the files were impossible to recover. Still, I read on.

By this point, my body was shaking so hard that I was in full-blown shock. I was nearly hyperventilating. I could barely type to do my internet searching. How could this be happening? This was my heart, my soul, on digital paper. It was everything that had given me the courage to finally say I was a "writer" and to start the blog and maybe even the book that so many had said I should. It was everything I felt the Lord had taught me, rescued me from, things I'd journaled about, and wanted to share...for 12 years.

It was after midnight when I went downstairs to the dark kitchen. I stood alone in the cold, the only light coming from the clock on the microwave. It felt dark in my soul, too. "Lord, why? These are words I wrote down because you told me to. You gave them to me. It's my testimony of what you've done in my life and the ways you've rescued, healed, and shown up. Yes, there are pages of raw words that will never see the light of day because they are too personal and painful to share, but I wrote them because you said to. These pages represent so much work and time spent with you, listening to you, waiting for you to speak."

Then, the Lord gently said, "Yes. And because of it, you know my voice. I put those words in you, and I will put them in you again. You are starting this new thing; it needs to come from a new place."

I stood there motionless. Blinking. And then I did the only thing I knew to do.

With my face wet and body shaking, I slowly laid face down in my kitchen and put my forehead on the floor. Through sobs that wracked my body, I gave those 394 files to the Lord.

I felt like Mary with her alabaster jar, pouring out every bit of what she had before the Lord. I didn't want to give up those files, but because the Lord and I had walked together through hard things before, and even though this didn't look the way I wanted it to, I knew His heart. I knew His voice. I knew He could be trusted.

All at once, I began hearing familiar choruses to worship songs echoing in my soul. Songs that sung the truth of Scripture, God's heart for me, and what was absolute about His character. Through those lyrics, He reminded me that surrender, though difficult, was the example He set with His own life, and one I knew I could follow.

Then, as if in a mysterious vision, I could see myself on the floor and the 394 files poured out all around me, carrying all the words I thought needed to be said. In that place of surrender, it was as if the sound of His voice reverberating in my ears turned into words and refilled all those pages with fresh words, thoughts and ideas. Then, those words flew off the pages, straight into my heart, ready to be used again, but this time, new. Not only new to me, but new in the way I heard, understood and articulated His voice.

Finally, after a few minutes, I heard myself say out loud, as if it wasn't me at all, "Okay Lord, make it new again."

Sometime later, I went upstairs and got in bed. Now, before you think I'm pious and holy and have Leviticus memorized, I need you to understand that when I went upstairs, I did not have an overwhelming peace. I was still so sad, and I didn't have any assurance of *anything* except *everything* was gone. However, I knew that the Lord was faithful and had been and would be. There was nothing more I could do.

At 3:15 a.m., my eyes popped open. It had only been about two hours. My waking thought was that my folder was gone, and I was instantly in tears. Then, just as fast, the refrain from all those worship songs came flooding back along with the reminder that He would make it all new.

At that moment, I have never felt more like Paul as he sat in prison. I was beaten and battered and in a prison of sadness and chained to the floor of my circumstance, and I knew I had to worship, or it would all cave in on me. So, I laid in bed and recounted back to God who He was, what He had done in my life, all the worship-infused bravery that I could muster, and every imaginable Scripture declaring victory. If I wasn't going to win, my heart wouldn't go down without a fight.

And then, without warning, those prison doors flew open.

Out of the blue, I had two ideas. I am, admittedly, a bit of a techy nerd. I knew that I could restore a backup from my phone that would then transfer to the computer via the cloud...and that just might work. If not, I could download a recovery program and do a back-end search of every possible keyword for possibly a few files to be restored. It was literally my last hope.

I started with the phone, that was low-hanging fruit. I found the last backup, erased and reset the phone, and restored it to sync with the cloud. Still nothing. Everything was still gone.

Meanwhile, my mind and heart were still trying to sing those songs in between me begging God through more tears to please make it all come back. I found and loaded a recovery program. This would be the last-ditch effort.

I took a deep breath and typed, "waiting on wonders." Nothing.

"blog posts." Nothing.

"transcripts." Nothing.

"writing folder." Nothing.

I closed the recovery program, uninstalled it, and stared at the completely blank desktop on my computer. There was nothing. It was all gone.

And then...there was something.

To my astonishment, a backup file from Time Machine opened and began to populate on the screen dated two days prior. All the missing files began to show up, one after another, right before my eyes.

Please remember. I had not set up the backup capabilities of Time Machine on my computer yet. (See the picture for proof!)

For the next five minutes, in the pitch black of my kitchen with just the light from my computer screen illuminating my red and swollen face, I watched all 394 files repopulate in their correct folders and categories and placement from a program that literally *did not exist* on my computer. I clapped my hand over my mouth, unsure if I would scream or throw up. I burst into tears again. All I could say over and over was, "Thank you. Thank you. Thank you. Thank you." By 4:15 am, all of the files were perfectly restored as if nothing had happened.

This is a long story. You deserve a medal for making it this far. But here is the pause:

The Lord didn't cause me to put that file in the trash, but He was willing to use that incredibly painful event in my life where I thought that everything I had worked for in my writing life up to that moment was for absolutely nothing, to teach me.

He used those hours, my war-worship, my honest lament, and raw emotion to show me something that has marked me: He's *better* and worth it all, and I know His voice better because I walked through this.

Had it all stayed the same, and the folder never shown back up, had those documents been vaporized in the mystical cloud forever, had the tears dried and the desk pounding produced only bruised hands, He still would have been better and so worth waiting on. Today, I have the privilege of knowing His voice better because of this paused moment with my forehead on the floor, surrendered with sobbing what belonged to Him anyway, and gave back to His loving hands what He wanted to use to help me write this book.

He's better than anything we think we could want, and He will use any situation in our lives to point us back to Him.

Are we listening? Fellow Wait-er...Are. We. Listening? I want to be. I want to know His voice in a crowd, in my garden, when I'm with my kids, and when I'm all alone in my kitchen. Whether in the very hard or most joyful moments, I want to be found listening.

Today, there's one thing I know for sure: every single day, God is speaking. Sometimes we just have to pause long enough to hear what He is saying.

Wait for and confidently expect the Lord; Be strong and
let your heart take courage;
Yes, wait for and confidently expect the Lord.
—
PSALM 27:14 (AMPC)

Much Love,

-TB

ACKNOWLEDGMENTS

Greg - I do. Again. Everyday. Amen. Thank you for the hours you've given so this could be real. You are my dream keeper. Now, let's go to Italy.

Ethan - You've always had a front-row seat to everything I don't know. Thank you for turning out great, regardless, and being the first precious wonder I ever wrote about.

Brody - Thank you for serving me day in and out with water, coffee, hugs, and laughter as I wrote this book upstairs. You are a gift to our family. You clearly get all your funny stuff from me.

Lydia - You are my favorite daughter-in-love and the perfect complement to Ethan. Thank you for supporting me in the writing, finding the perfect spot for the spark, and always choosing to share my words with your world. Hugs.

Mom/Dad/Tori/Tré - I never intended to be a writer, but regardless, there is Honey Creek and Harvest Drive in everything I say. Thank you for being the first ones to love me and always being the loudest cheerleaders.

Julie/Liz/Mamie - You are my people. Thank you for late-night dinners and raw words and laughing until Mamie holds her nose and snorts. You are the real true ones.

Garrett/Brandon - All of your ideas are good ones. Challenging me to write this book just might be the best idea you've ever had. Without you, I wouldn't have started. Thank you.

AnnaJaye - For 6:15 a.m. conversations that crafted so much commentary, "Citizens of Heaven" is for you.

Jan - Every writer has an ideal audience. You are mine. Thank you for being excited...about everything, even on a Tuesday.

Kathy - For loving me enough to ask me all the hard questions and always wanting to bring me pens and water.

PG - For being the first to ask, "What is God saying to you and what are you going to do about it?" Thank you for teaching me how to pause and reflect.

Seacoast Church - Thank you for being such a healthy house where I have been able to grow up, learn under incredible leadership, and worship with joy.

Seacoast Worship Family - Thank you for listening to me ramble about these things in green rooms and on platforms and at Family Tree. Being with you makes me better and it is my honor to worship with you.

Leigh - October 1, 2016 changed my life. Thank you for being bold enough to invite me to speak and believe for my healing that day. So much of your friendship and support is woven into these words. I write today from a sound mind and whole body, thanks be to God.

Supper Club - For being the first to know about the book, hear and cheer. For the last two years, you have made my literal dreams come true. Thank you for fighting for it.

Chosen Lead team - For believing in this thing, maybe even more than I did. Thank you for the honor of the platform. I'm still undone by your kindness.

Carrie - For creating the selah spark and the most beautiful cover to wrap up all my words. Your art is a gift to the world and your heart and friendship, a treasure to me.

Marney - For taking on the task of wrangling all my words with grace and making them so much better. I'm so grateful for your willingness and expertise.

Typewriter Creative - For believing in this project and being so wonderful to work with. Your creativity is the gift I didn't know I needed.

Kaua'i County - Nou ko'u pu'uwai. Mahalo iā 'oe no ka ho'okipa mau 'ana ia'u, a hā'awi mai ia'u i wahi e hanu ai a ho'olohe i ka Haku.

The Wait-ers - This book has been writing *me* for the last 12 years. Thank you for being as excited about it as I am. Thank you for reading the blog, subscribing, commenting, reposting Instagram posts, and sharing with your friends. Thank you to the Launch Team for being behind the vision, encouraging me along the way, and pushing me to get my words in the world. No matter how our paths crossed, I want each of you to know how grateful I am for your support. As you wait on the Lord and listen for His voice, remember that He is crazy about you and so excited for you to discover Him in the daily. I thank you for coming alongside and waiting on wonders with me.

ABOUT

Tara L. Banks has been secretly writing behind her computer screen for the last 12 years. It wasn't until she decided to write her first book and then accidentally lost every word she'd ever written that she knew the topic had to be what God was teaching her through everyday moments like that one. While happiest behind that screen, writing on Instagram, or her blog, *Waiting on Wonders*, she enjoys speaking on podcasts and at events, and sharing her experiences through mentoring and coaching. Tara is a worship pastor at Seacoast Church in Mount Pleasant, South Carolina. She also is COO of the social-good lifestyle brands CARMIN BLACK, and its partnering non-profit, HALF UNITED, which together fight hunger and help people in need. She is married to her college sweetheart, Greg, and they have two sons, Ethan and Brody, and a daughter-in-love, Lydia. When she is not tinkering with her '73 CJ-5 Jeep or dreaming of Hawaii, you will more than likely find her waiting on wonders...

WAITINGONWONDERS.COM

Made in United States
Orlando, FL
02 May 2023

32730241R00080